BUDDHA YOGA

Prof Thich Hue Dang

DIAMOND BOOKS

www.diamondbook.in

Co-Publisher:
Dr. Biswaroop Roy Chowdhury

Published By:
Diamond Pocket Books
X-30, Okhla Industrial Area, Phase-II
New Delhi-110020
Ph.: 011-40712200
E-mail: sales@dpb.in Website: www.diamondbook.in

TABLE OF CONTENTS

FOREWORD

Having had the pleasure of being associated with Prof Thich Hue Dang has been one of the greatest ever. A learned man, he comes from a lifetime of experience and with the knowledge he has acquired over decades.

This book written by this truly wise man, who has reached the level of having a Buddha mind is a must read for anyone in the pursuit of Buddhayoga.

In this book, Prof Thich Hue Dang talks about his life journey and achievements in a way that every reader can instantly draw a connection with the book, and hence with him.

I wish all the readers of this book success on their paths to achieving the Buddha mind through the yoga methods talked about in this book.

Regards
Dr Biswaroop Roy Chowdhury

PART I:

INTRODUCTION TO THE PRACTICE AND PRACTICAL RESULTS OF PROFESSOR THICH HUE DANG

If we want to achieve inner wisdom, we must study the paths of the Mahasiddhas (people with great achievements) because the life of a Mahasiddha has to go through many difficult and arduous journeys that require a continuous effort to attain wisdom. Therefore, I also found and learned the roadmap for applying Buddha's wisdom to life based on the practice and practical results of the Mahasiddhas.

In India, in the olden times, most gurus and practitioners followed the Vedas sutra, including practicing yoga. Shakyamuni Buddha also meditated using yogic methods to gain mind power. He practiced the three advanced yoga disciplines of Kriyâ Yoga, Sushuma Yoga, and Chakra Yoga that practitioners use to open the inner sources of human beings.

I.Methods to practice yoga

Through my own practical experiences, I have seen this path. I was fortunate to meet my master who taught me Kriyâ Yoga and

Sushuma Yoga. At that time, I did not know these two disciplines had also been practiced by Shakyamuni Buddha.

I practiced these yoga methods in a cave in Thien Cam Mountain. This practice is called the 'Merging yourself with universe', which is when the universal energy gets united with the body all the way from the top of the head to the bottom of the foot of practitioners. It is about merging the Yin and the Yang energy flows.

After three years of practicing in the cave, I left the mountain and began studying and researching documents that were published before 1975. It was then that I discovered that the methods that I had cultivated while practicing on the mountain were the famous Kriyâ Yoga and Sushuma Yoga of India.

Then, I set off on a journey where I wandered from the Mekong Delta to Saigon all alone to find my direction in life. I asked myself, *'What next? I have cultivated the Kriyâ yoga, Sushumna yoga and have already got into Samadhi, so what should I do now?'*

II. Searching for Buddha's philosophy

I searched for Buddha's philosophy everywhere, but I did not meet anyone who understood the philosophy of Buddha. I went to the temples and pagodas in Mekong Delta and Saigon, but I did not find what I was searching for a number of years.

Finally, I was fortunate to meet a friend who gave me a book called 'The Secret Tantra of Tibet' which mentioned the Chakra yoga. I discovered that Shakyamuni Buddha also practiced these three types of yoga. This book, which is written in French, talked only about the theory of Chakra yoga and its results, but not about the practice techniques. In this book, it is said that if you want to open your chakras, you have to go through the two previous paths, one is Kriyâ yoga and the other is Sushumna yoga, and must have a path to open it. After studying, I found a way to combine these three disciplines. I decided to go into a closed room for 49 long days to open my chakras. After that, I returned to Vung Tau to continue my practice for another two years to complete my Chakra yoga practice.

It was a blessing that I was naturally lead on a planned path, which included the complete system of the three disciplines of Kriyâ yoga, Sushumna yoga and Chakra yoga. These three disciplines are within our body, and not outside. Even if one of these three methods is missing in our practice, this system does not remain systematic and we cannot open all inner sources of body.

I completed the yoga methods which were practiced by Buddha. I thought, 'If I practice the methods practiced by Buddha without knowing or understanding his philosophy, then how can I apply it?' That is when I decided to go to Dong Nai to become a monk at Long Thien Meditation pagoda. I took refuge with the Most Venerable Thich Hue Thanh, and received the Bhikkhu precepts.

Even though I had entered Samadhi, had been ordained and lived in the temple, I always felt uncomfortable in my heart and felt that I still had not found the key to the application of Buddha's philosophy. Once I studied the Vimalakirti Buddha Sutra, I realized the meaning behind these two sentences:

"Without leaving Buddhism while doing ordinary jobs is the ultimate state of true mind.

Not being deep down into the highest state of Samadhi while presenting its majestic power is the ultimate state of true mind"

In 1983, I decided to ask Venerable Hue Thanh to leave Long Thien pagoda to go back into life. I left the pagoda with empty hands. I went to Da Lat to practice and get practical results, which I get till date. Before leaving the Patriarch, the Venerable Hue Thanh said to me, *"If a monk leaves the pagoda, he cannot be successful. If a tiger leaves the mountain he cannot survive."* Regardless, I decided to leave and start walking my own path.

III. Enlighten my own True mind

I came to Da Lat with empty hands. The living conditions were very difficult and I had to go through with the hardships. At that time, I saw that the farmers had to quit growing Cymbidiums, because they could not export it. I collected the orchids that were thrown away. On To Hien Thanh Street, there was a vegetable market. Early in the morning, I would go to the market to pick up the vegetables that were cut off and brought them back home to eat. I planted orchids to live, and silently practiced Buddha meditation. Once I was in my sleep, I was opened the wisdom of Buddha for seven days and nights, which was mentioned in the Lotus Sutra by Buddha. I realized that was the wisdom of Buddha which is called the true mind, Buddhahood or Buddha mind is present in every human being. Since then, I made this state of mind the basis for my practice and application.

In the philosophy of Vajrayana sutra, it is said that application of emptiness and compassion is honesty and Loving kindness. The application of emptiness and compassion is the application of the true mind.

How can we achieve True mind to gain wisdom?

The key practice of the Buddha yoga philosophy is transforming our consciousness into Buddha wisdom and apply it to life in order to get practical results. To gain Buddha wisdom, you must understand the Prajna sutra. It was because of this that before entering Nirvana, Buddha passed his wisdom to his great student Mahakassapa; "I passed to you the truth of the eyes, the Nirvana and Wisdom." Nirvana is the Buddha mind, Buddhahood, pure mind or true mind. Wisdom is the application intuition from Buddha mind. The key practice to get wisdom is by applying the mind of sacrifice, patience, diligence, honesty and compassion. It was left to us in the Buddha philosophy.

In 1993, I wrote an explanation to my Venerable Master, Thich Hue Thanh about the way to transform our consciousness to Buddha wisdom and how to train Vajrayana students. Two months later, I received a letter from him confirming that I was on the right path of the Buddhas and the Patriarchs, as a successful Zen master who had passed, the path of the body and breathing practice with Kriyâ Yoga, Sushumna Yoga, and Chakra Yoga and mind practice. He ordered me to continue preaching to the community. With the help of the Venerable Master, I went to study two Buddha philosophy lecturer training courses for seven years.

Looking back at my path of practice, I realized that I had practiced the mind of sacrifice, patience, and diligence. The mind of self-sacrifice was when I renounced my family. I patiently practiced meditation and got practical results by selling orchids, writing books, giving sermons, and planting and producing Ngoc Linh ginseng. I was taught by no one about the practical path of Buddha or the true mind. I naturally went on the right path to the true mind as Buddha taught.

I began my teaching career in 1994. After that, in 2004, the Central Committee of Vietnam Buddhist Sangha sent me to Europe to teach in five countries – Belgium, Germany, France, Italy and Netherlands. In 2005, I was invited to the United States to teach the Lankavatara Sutra and the Vimalakirti Sutra.

IV. Verifying results and achievements in life

1. To be recognized by Harvard (USA) as an intellectual person

To Thich Hue Dang –

A man – but no ordinary man. A man I trust immediately who spoke wisdom to me at a critical time in my life.

With my thanks & respect –

Alex S. Jones

Vào ngày 6/12/2011, tại Hà Nội, đã diễn ra buổi gặp thân mật giữa Thầy Thích Huệ Đăng và ông Alex Jones – Giám đốc Trung tâm Truyền thông, Chính trị và Chính sách công thuộc Đại học Harvard (Hoa Kỳ).

Sau một vài giờ trao đổi, ông Alex S. Jones cảm kích với những chia sẻ của Thầy về trí tuệ và ông đã viết kính tặng Thầy những lời chân thành để bày tỏ sự biết ơn và kính trọng. Dưới đây là bản dịch nội dung những dòng cảm xúc của ông:

Kính gửi Ngài Thích Huệ Đăng.

Ngài không phải là một người bình thường!

Tôi đã tin tưởng Ngài ngay khi gặp gỡ và Ngài đã chia sẻ cho tôi hiểu về trí tuệ vào một thời điểm vô cùng quan trọng trong cuộc đời của tôi.

Với lòng biết ơn và kính trọng.

Alex S. Jones

2. Awarded the Certificate of Merit by the Minister of Science and Technology of Vietnam to recognize contributions in the field of scientific research

3. To be a Lecturer in the Vietnam Buddhist Sangha

- Recognized as a lecturer of Propagation of faith (Buddhism) of Vietnam Buddhist Sangha under the document No.1941/GCN/BHP/HDTS, dated 24 August 1999 of the Management Board of Vietnam Buddhist Sangha (Attached document in appendices)- Graduated the advanced course of the Central Dharma Propagation Committee of the Vietnam Buddhist Sangha Graduation date: 28 December 2004, course period: 2001 – 2004
- Member of Vietnam Buddhist Research Institute
- Wrote and published 43 Sutras Lecturing sets and Sutras Interpretation books approved and licensed by Religion Publishing House.

4. To be recognized as the Master of Yoga

- Practiced three advanced yoga disciplines: Kriya Yoga, Sushumna Yoga, Chakra Yoga for nearly 50 years. Those are three yoga disciplines that have nearly been lost in the world.
- Granted the title of Master of Yoga (documents attached in appendices) by The International Sivananda Yoga Vedanta Center under the Vedanta Forest Yoga Academy (headquartered in Quebee Jot 2Ro, Canada)

5. To preserve and develop Ngoc Linh ginseng in Vietnam

- Summer of 2008: Climbed up to Ngoc Linh Mountain (Kon Tum Province) with two students to research the implementation of the tissue culture method to breed Ngoc Linh ginseng (Attachment document appendix)- October 2012: Awarded by the National Office of Intellectual Property of the Ministry of Science and Technology (No. 10798) for the Patent for 'The process of breeding Ngoc Linh ginseng by tissue culture method'; confirmed as 'The First Scientist of Vietnamese Buddhism' by Governmental Religion Board (Attachment document appendix).
- 2013: Established the Vietnam Ngoc Linh Ginseng Investment Joint Stock Company- 2015: Successfully produced the product of Ngoc Linh ginseng biomass extraction in the form of tablets, supporting the treatment of diseases related to liver, lung, diabetes and cancer.
- 2017: Cooperated with the Vietnam Institute of Science and Technology to experiment and apply nanotechnology in the production of Ngoc Linh ginseng biomass extraction, boosting the quantity and quality of products, being in the clinical period and has got very positive results.

6. Establishing and administering the Institute of Vietnam Buddha Yoga Research and Application

- Established the 'Institute of Vietnam Buddha Yoga Research and Application' under Decision No. 1007/QD-VHTHVN dated 19 December 2016 of the Vietnam Union of Science and Technology Associations, Certificate of Science and Technology Activities No. A-1693 dated 27 December 2016 of the Ministry of Science and Technology, the author is appointed as Director of the Institute (Attachment document for appendix). This is the first time that the Buddha's philosophy has been recognized by the highest level among Vietnam governmental management offices on science and technology.

- Established four Buddha Yoga Centers in Vietnam, one center in Hanoi, one center in Ba Ria - Vung Tau, two centers in Da Lat - Lam Dong to organize the training in four steps: Student - Teacher - Trainer - Senior Trainer - Master.
- Cooperated with the Yoga Alliance in the training of teachers and trainers of Vietnam Buddha Yoga according to international standards (attached documents in appendices).

7. Vietnam Book of Records (Vietkings) awards Vietnam record as

'The first monk who is the author of the patent granted in Vietnam' to Venerable Thich Hue Dang (Real name: NGUYEN VAN SAU)

8. The Global Education Record Holder Institute (GERI) awards certificate of Honorary Professor to Record Holder Nguyen Van Sau on May 21, 2018

9. The World Records Content Academy (WRCA)

World Records Union (WorldKings) received the nomination from Vietnam Book of Records (Vietkings) for the profile of record holder Nguyen Van Sau. WRCA's Committee granted record content of dedication to Mr. Nguyen Van Sau on April 30, 2018 and recognized him as 'not only a monk of Buddhism but also a scientist who has a great contribution and dedication to Vietnamese Social Community'.

10. World Records University

Awarded the Honorary Doctorate for the title 'The first monk who is an author and a scientist granted an exclusive patent in Vietnam' on August 26, 2018.

11. On September 26, 2018, the **Institute of Science and Technology for Economic and Culture Development** awarded the gold table to register: Vietnam Gold Businessmen in 2018

12. December 26, 2019: Received an international award in India

13. December 27, 2019: Received an Honorary Professor Degree by the World Records University Institute.

PART II:

APPLYING THE PHILOSOPHY OF BUDDHA

I. PRACTICAL EXPERIENCE OF PROFESSOR THICH HUE DANG

1. Biography

Over forty-five years of my practice, I realized that the life of a human being has many ups and downs. I want to share with you the ups and downs of my religious life and my science experience.

I was born in 1940 in Ho Chi Minh City (formerly called Saigon). My parents died early (my father died when I was 9 years old and my mother when I was 12), I only finished the third grade in a village school. We have four schools in our life: The first school is family which I never really had. The second is school is the public, which again I did not have. The third school is religion; and the fourth is the real-life school. I did not have two schools: family and public schools. When I was thirty-two years old, I began to find a direction for my own life, so I went on to practice yoga.

My practice was different than that of Vietnamese Buddhist monks. I was fortunate to return to Cam Mountain - Chau Doc, where I practiced yoga in the cave. I practiced Kriya yoga and Sushumna yoga methods that were lost over 1000 years in

India. I practiced for less than three years. I was searching for my own path. After that, I asked my master to return to Ho Chi Minh City to find a new direction. Once, I came across a book in French which was called 'Basic Tibetan Tantra'. I asked a French professor to help me translate the book to Vietnamese. In that book, it said: a Tantric Yogacara practitioner must have Chakra yoga. So, I decided to continue with this path.

I went to Vung Tau and entered the closed room for two years to learn and perfect the Chakra yoga. After doing so, I went to meet Venerable Hue Thanh. He was the Vice-Master of the Central Proven Council of Vietnam Buddhist Sangha. I left home and became a monk. After that, I joint Buddhism lecturer courses. It took me 7 years for studying and teaching. After finishing these courses, the Vietnam Buddhist Sangha sent me to India for two more years to study Sanskrit. I researched and practiced a lot more about Tibetan Tantra.

2. People have endless resources

I trust the Vietnamese people very much. But why do I trust Vietnamese people? Because I started from a third-grade student in a village school, how can I become a Buddhist lecturer and succeed in science?

Eight years ago, I was asked by the Political Communication Director of Harvard University to visit Vietnam for dialogue for three hours. He hugged me and shed tears, he wrote me a document: 'On December 6, 2011, an informal meeting took place in Hanoi between Mr. Thich Hue Dang and Mr. Alex John

- Director of Harvard Center for Communication, Politics and Public Policy (USA). After a few hours of exchange, Mr. Alex S. Jones appreciated the tears of his intellectual share of humanity. And he wrote to me these sincere words to express his gratitude and respect. Below is the content translation of Alex Jones's emotional line:

To Thich Hue Dang

A man but not an ordinary man!

A man to trust immediately who shared wisdom with me at a critical time in my life.

With thanks and respect Alex S. Jones

Human beings have an intellectual and wise mind. The intellectual one is based on qualifications and knowledge from outside. Even a doctorate one is still limited in intellectual boundary. When it comes to the Buddha wisdom, one does not need a degree to prove his achievement as long as he achieves his true mind as it then that his wisdom will emerge. Sakyamuni Buddha, also known as Siddhārtha Gautama, was the son of King Śuddhodana, a martial arts master and well-educated prince. But he refused the heir throne. Gautama quit his palace for the life of a mendicant. He spent five years looking for the enlightenment and six years living in asceticism, and then brought the bowl to beg for alms for forty-nine years. What was his purpose? He practiced his own mind, completed his own wisdom.

In May 2018, I was invited to join a training course with the theme 'turning record resources into valuable assets' by the

Vietnam Book of Records. Why did they invite me to participate? They looked for me and understood my way. They knew that I was a monk and a scientist. Harvard University had confirmed that I was a wise man.

The process of my study of Ngoc Linh ginseng was extremely arduous; there was no harvest for eight years. I had to sell orchids in order to get some money to maintain my Ginseng research. This process started in 2008, when I went to Ngoc Linh Mountain, 2800 meters high, and found ninety-eight ginsengs. I brought them home for tissue culture. In 2012, I was granted the first patent of the National Office of Intellectual Property under the Ministry of Science and Technology for the process of growing Ngoc Linh ginseng for tissue culture method. On May 15, 2018, I was awarded the second exclusive patent for the Ngoc Linh ginseng extract tablet.

Once again, I repeat, I believe in Vietnamese people very much. Why am I so confident? King Tran Nhan Tong defeated the Mongolian army twice. The Mongolian army had occupied all of Eastern Europe, but when came to Vietnam, they had to stop. The story of King Tran Nhan Tong was set in the 16th century, and in the 21st century, President Ho Chi Minh is also said to be a wise man. At that time, our people were poor and backward, and the French and the Americans had the supreme weapons, but how did we push these two powers out of Vietnam? This made me question about my life a lot. For this reason, I decided to find my own path.

I was at Long Thien Church for 10 years. After that, I asked my master (Venerable Thich Hue Thanh) to leave the pagoda to get back to life. I was back to life but was not to get married. I practiced the Buddha philosophy in real life. I went to Da Lat, I studied orchids, I implanted tissue and I succeeded. I wanted to do something for the community. So, I practiced three vows: 'Taking the true mind as my father, taking wisdom as my mother, and taking the community as my family'. I was not a highly educated person; how can I study science? I was granted by the Ministry of Science to obtain two exclusive patent licenses and to be the Director of Institute of Vietnam Buddha Yoga Research and Application. I prove that Buddhism is a religion of wisdom. Buddhism is a religion of science. Buddhism is a religion of the community. I confirm to you, I am responsible towards the Vietnam Buddhist Sangha, towards my master, Shakyamuni Buddha and for my words.

3. Think back on your life

Previously, I presented that people have intellectual and wisdom parts. Wisdom comes from the true mind of the human being.

I was a lecturer in Soc Son University for three years and Van Hanh University for two years. I preached in Australia, Europe and the United States. I was always looking for people who could achieve the Buddha wisdom.

I say so, can we all review whether it is correct or not?

Shakyamuni discovered the wisdom path more than 2500 years ago; how do we follow this path too?

Why does the United Nations recognize the Buddhist truth of humanity?

Why does the United Nations recognize yoga of humanity, not only India?

I was very anxious, because I was 80 years old, my health deteriorated, what could I do?

I have three goals to spread: Buddhism philosophy, Buddha yoga and Ngoc Linh ginseng.

The first is Buddhism philosophy. I wrote the first 43 Buddhism books in Vietnamese, in which there are 21 commentaries and 22 interpretations of the Mahayana sutras. They help people understand the Buddhism philosophy.

The second is Buddha yoga which includes the Kriya yoga, Sushumna yoga and Chakra yoga which had been lost in the world for nearly 1,000 years. I was recognized by an international yoga institute headquartered in Canada as Master of yoga. I was fully ordained and got the Ordinary licenses as a Swami under Vedic sutra. Vedic Sutra is India's greatest sutra, which included yoga.

The third one is Ngoc Linh ginseng. In 1983, scientists from Ngoc Linh Ginseng Center researched, but they had not yet succeeded. They could not perform the tissue culture containing MR2 in the lab. Now, I can make it and produce it in compressed pills.

I believe in Vietnamese people. How can Vietnamese people gain wisdom? I proved it through King Tran Nhan Tong and Ho Chi Minh. So, what must we do in this life? Do you understand what it is for? I share a few things for all of us to have a review, to re-examine our lives.

Institute of Vietnam Buddha Yoga Research and Application is now in Lam Dong, Tuyen Lam Lake tourist area. We have forty-five engineers who have been trained by me. From 4:30 am to 8:00 pm, the students are both studying and working. They implant and make Ngoc Linh ginseng pills, and then practice yoga and Buddha Philosophy. I established a Dharma Realm of Five Buddhism Mahayana. I opened four yoga centers, two in Lam Dong, one in Hanoi, one in Ba Ria where they practice yoga and they give lectures. They teach yoga to everyone. The Buddha said: Health is the most valuable property of mankind. So, by bringing the yoga to community, you bring good health to everyone. In the Institute of Vietnam Buddha Yoga Research and Application, I take three goals as the target for my training methods: health, skill and prestige. People who have good health can practice to have skills. You apply your skills to serve the community. I am eager to ask you to have a trust in the family and let the community trust you to contribute to the development of the country. We must understand that wisdom must have practical results in real life, to be honest and to be recognized by the community.

And people who get practical results for the community have three things: The first is to leave a work, the second is to leave a precious tree and the third is to train a person.

4. The roadmap for human resource training starts from practicing to gain practical results.

The methodology of training human resource is: Sacrifice - Patience – Diligence- Honesty and Compassion.

I have taken the example of all three wise men: The first is the example of Shakyamuni Buddha, my master; the second is the example of King Tran Nhan Tong; and the third is the example of Ho Chi Minh. These three people all went on a three-minded route: The first is to have a mind of sacrifice, the second is to have a mind of patience, and the third is to have a diligent mind.

I wrote a commentary of the journey to the consciousness of human beings. There are eight consciousnesses. The seventh is the mind-attachment that humans should accept negativity and suffering. The eighth is the one containing all information. This is like a CPU; the past and the present information is all saved here. If we can use the mind of sacrifice, patience and diligence, then we can turn the intellectual knowledge into wisdom.

How do we deal with others? We should treat others with honesty and compassion. I conclude that if we live with five minds: sacrifice, patience, diligence, honesty and compassion, we will succeed in any field. That is the wisdom application roadmap.

Use wisdom to train people and to develop skills in any area. People who have wisdom will succeed in life.

I grow orchids and sell orchids to make money to grow ginseng. I produce Ngoc Linh ginseng compressed pills with forty-five workers. From 2008 to 2017, I sold ginseng tablets to raise money to pay to the students. I went to sell orchids in the middle of the market in 23/9 park. Why do I have to do that? Because I want to practice patience and I want to practice sacrifice. This is why my teacher, Sakyamuni, brought a bowl to beg for alms for 49 years. He did not have any shortage of food, he did not lack money, but he went on this path for mind practice. I thought I studied his documents, so I decided to leave the pagoda. Although, at that time, I was the manager of the Vassa School (Buddhist summer school) with 250 monks and nuns. I had left it all to go to grow orchids, sell orchids, and sleep in the market. Five years ago, a journalist came to see me. He saw me carrying orchid pots for people, and then taking the money from customers. He met me and asked:

"Teacher, why does a monk go to the market, why do not you stay in the pagoda for spiritual practice?"

I answered, "Hey, do not lose your true mind while earning and using money."

He looked at me and said, "Teacher, can I ask you a question? If a monk grows and sells orchids, then how can he have the time for spiritual practice?"

I just answered, "Taking the cold wind on street to understand your mind. Taking the up and down steps of life to train your mind is all a part of the spiritual practice."

He stood for about ten minutes and said, "Teacher, let me ask you another question. Are your answers following the words of Shakyamuni Buddha?"

He clearly did not know the Buddha Sutra, so I just simply answered by saying. "If you do not go into real life, what do you take to train yourselves? If you do not study Buddha philosophy, how do you know to train your mind?"

I go into life to practice Buddha philosophy. Buddha has said two sentences:

"Not being deep into highest state of Samadhi while presenting its majestic power is the ultimate state of true mind"

"Not showing the Samadhi form but presenting its power, it is the true mind."

Buddha is the stage of true mind. You achieve it and must apply it in real life because only the real life can help you to train your mind.

I would like to repeat, I want to send a message to everyone, living in life must have a heart of sacrifice. Sacrifice what? Sacrifice your selfishness, greed, jealousy, lies, ego, laziness and pride. When we are faced with difficulties and obstacles, we must be steadfast and patient to overcome it and succeed. My medicine factory was burnt in the beginning of April last year. I was about to close the company, but one of my students called in and said, "Teacher, 45 children are studying and working diligently. Do not close the company. If you close the company, we will not have a place to study and practice." So, we keep going forward.

Why do we try our best to be successful? Is it for being famous or having money? No, I do that to train myself and students through applying in business. I do it to open my own mind, train my own mind, train people and to bring benefits to the community.

4. What are the key messages of this book?

As I mentioned above about the endless sources of human beings that help me be successful in life without any higher education.

Recently, I presented that people have intellectual and wisdom parts. Wisdom comes from the true mind of the human being, which is also called Buddhahood.

The first: The operation principles of human consciousness

The second: Buddhahood, the primitive pure mind of human beings

The third: Practicing sacrifice, patience, diligence, honesty and compassion to transforming from using consciousness to Buddhahood wisdom with these 5 mind rituals

The fourth: The application methods in everyday life. It is included many meditation techniques to help you to develop and apply the wisdom of Buddha mind to daily life.

II: THE IMPORTANCE OF HEALTH - SKILLS - PRESTIGE

Talking about training a person to practice and gain practical results, this is really a very difficult issue. I have taken the material from an application book of the Institute of Vietnam Buddha Yoga Research and Application to give the community a living message. People need three basic things to have a peaceful and happy life: health - wisdom (skills) - prestige.

The practical results are proof of a process of trying regardless of day and night. People must have health to be able to achieve the skills and to do all the work. These skills (wisdom) are obtained from the true peace of mind. When we have health, we gain skills; we can gain credibility with the action. And when it comes to prestige, it also means that the process of arduous practice has been rewarded with practical, useful for the community.

Buddha once said that health is the property of mankind. When we were young, we took our health and sold them to exchange money. When we get old, can we give money to buy our health back? Now, if we offer money in exchange for health, who will give us health again? We must know the value of what I just said. If not, we will throw away our own life in sickness.

After I succeeded, I contemplated my route. So, I pointed out three criteria for the institute: health - wisdom (skills) - prestige. I find that these three criteria are the most valuable assets of a person.

In the process of training skills, there must be a mind of sacrifice, patience and diligence. Without these three minds, the skill will not be achieved. And true love is the foundation of a happy life. Sacrifice, patience and diligence will help us succeed, but they must be accompanied by honesty and compassion. Because, there is no sacrifice, patience, diligence and success, there will be no honesty and compassion. Then, you will always live in anxiety, suffering, and will not have freedom.

I am 81 years old but I am in good health, thanks to the skills (wisdom) to achieve science, and I have a prestige for the community. With health, skills and prestige, your life can be peaceful and happy. This roadmap has no discrimination, no matter how we look, no matter what religion we follow, no matter what kind of culture we have; if we have this roadmap, we will gain achievement. And the motivation and the deepest goals of human life are also to achieve this goal.

Institute of Vietnam Buddha Yoga Research and Application sets these criteria as the training target.

I think a lot about the life we are living. We are growing in science and technology, materially, but we are facing diseases of body and soul, polluted environment, poisoned food, fake medicines, people living in deception, killing each other for their own benefit, regardless of possible consequences. I see more and more people leaving the happiness and peace in their own hearts.

As people in society tend to be more materialistic and distant, they lose both compassion and honesty. Each person becomes lonelier with his ego. All is due to the selfish and greedy mind. We are losing our true heart and compassion.

In such an era, those who recognize selfish deception and a meaningless life begin to rediscover the meaning of their own life, to find peace and happiness in their hearts by means of bring health - skills - prestige to benefit themselves and the community. People who live like that will achieve happiness.

So, is there a roadmap to follow? Who can train us here?

We must always ask ourselves: What are we in this life for? Is it for living a dishonest life? Are we here for cheating? What do we live for while our money will eventually be left behind?

We come to this point; can we please review our heart? See if our soul is generous or selfish?

I often advise students: Which path are you going on? What are you studying here? What are you practicing? What are you doing? You have to review to develop health, skills and prestige.

So, I created the Institute of Vietnam Buddha Yoga Research and Application for that purpose. Our goal is to bring health to the community through practicing methods. Yoga will give us good health. The only and most prerequisite condition is that we must work hard, exercise persistence and make continuous efforts, and we can acquire good health.

As a yoga master, I grasp the key of what is the most important to a human being's life, contributing to training a person who benefits for himself, the community and the country.

For example: I am a monk but at the same time I am the owner of two businesses (Thanh Quang Orchid Limited Company and Vietnam Ngoc Linh Ginseng Join Stock Company). I always think about my employees. They are also my students. I have a lot of compassion for them because they sacrificed their health to help me develop two companies without thinking of space and time. So, I set up yoga classes for them to practice from 6:30 am to 7:30 pm, help them recover their health, work better and more effectively. I have a thought: If all the business owners of Vietnam and the world can organize something like this for their employees, the world will be much better place. If the owner can do that, he does know how to use money, "Do not lose your true mind while earning and using money."

I would like to emphasize once more, if you want to be healthy, you must practice yoga.

Yoga is a method of body training (body practice), followed by the breathing (the breath practice), finally the mind practice (to obtain the inner power, the mind power, the wisdom power).

Currently, yoga is being chosen by the whole world as a method of exercise for health. Yoga is applied to the roadmap body practice, breath practice and mind practice of Institute of Vietnam Buddha Yoga Research and Application. Body practice is to practice yoga postures, also known as Asanas, to release toxins and have a strong, flexible body. Breathing practice is Mantra Yoga, Meditation and three yoga methods (Kriya Yoga, Sushumna Yoga and Chakra Yoga) to gain inner power. For mind practice, we apply philosophy of Buddha to have the power of wisdom.

With Buddha's philosophy, if we know how to practice, we will achieve Buddha's wisdom. Then, we bring this wisdom to apply into serving community we will improve as well as achieve skills. It is because Buddhism is the science of wisdom. At this point, we will be recognized by the community and will gain more prestige.

Buddha is the true mind.

Why did I create Buddha Yoga?

Why did Buddha, who used to be a prince choose this path?

Why did he give up all the golden palace, emeralds, beautiful wife, and good child to search for happiness in his true mind?

What is the basic philosophy of Buddha? How do we have this philosophy?

The Buddha did not leave money or a great Buddha temple, all he left behind was a means to bring people to their own true mind. Because anyone has this true mind, from within this true mind wisdom (skills) is manifested (by practicing sacrifice - patience - diligent mind). If we apply these skills to practice and gain practical results, we will have prestige in the community.

Through my experience of practice and experience for more than 45 years, to with draw the exact route to teach people how to apply in this life is five-minded practice: The mind of sacrifice, the mind of patience, the mind of diligence, the honesty and compassion. From here we go through awareness, intuition and enlightenment.

People who go on the road of mind 'sacrifice- patience- diligence' to transfer from an intellectual state of mind to the wisdom of true mind to practice in life can achieve practical results.

In order to have practice and practical results, we need four conditions: methods, means, human resource and location. Method is the application skills taught by a person. Means is finance. Human resource is your team. Location is your environment; there must be a good place to study and work to achieve health - skills - prestige.

Therefore, the Buddha has left us the philosophy of how to enter the true mind and how to apply the true mind wisdom into life. In the Mahaparinirvana Sutra, he said, "The night before I became enlightened, the following night I entered Nirvana and in the interval in between, I did not say a word." He only left to Mahakassapa - his great student- "Nirvana- eternal peace and wisdom of true mind." Thanks to that, I now have a teaching method to teach my students the 5 Mahayana of Buddhism in a dharma that has methods, means, human resource and location.

So now, how do we study and apply the Buddha philosophy? What is our path of life?

In the 21st century, we cannot do as what Buddha had done. We must go into life, do science and business to cultivate the mind of sacrifice - patience - diligence.

These three minds must be practiced daily. We need a master to teach us how to practice. If we are too greedy for food, sleep, money, fame and desire, our mind will be tied up and will develop to a higher stage. The more we get the more we leave behind because we cannot bring anything with us but our karma.

How should we treat other people? The answer is with Honesty and Compassion.

I have practiced the Buddha philosophy for more than 45 years and I can tell you that it only takes five steps – sacrifice - patience – diligence – honesty- compassion to make a journey to apply in life towards wisdom and enlightenment. So, I want to share these life messages and practical results with the community.

Wisdom must be proved by doing, practicing and getting practical results. It is clearly recognized by the community. It must have practical value, not only on paper. Enlightenment is also needed to be proved by works and community recognition, and not by words. Practicing these five steps help you to be matured, achieve enlightenment, wisdom and skills in life.

Once again, through many years of experience on the way of my practice and application, I summarized it into a clear, concise, easy-to-understand and easy-to-apply roadmap to help the community quickly fulfil their own practice.

Sacrifice - Patience – Diligence- Honesty – Compassion

This is the shortcut. It points directly to the true mind to see your own nature and reach Buddhahood and achieve wisdom. This is the secret of tantric enlightenment. Enlightenment is going straight to the true mind; the wisdom from this unconscious mind will arises. Then we apply into life and are recognized by the community. That is Buddha wisdom.

I have been through hardships to prove that this roadmap is valuable and meaningful for a human being's life. I really believe that Vietnamese people will continue on this route after I die.

Taking a path with a great heart will lead to great wisdom; great wisdom leads to great virtue; great virtue leads to great means; great means leads to great prestige; great prestige leads to great community, and great community leads great peace and happiness.

I was very anxious when I created such a roadmap, but I had confidence that my students will be able to go on this route. This is your own path, the unselfish path which helps yourselves and community.

I decided that in the last years of my life, I would like to utilize the achievements of my life to serve the community with all my heart. I will open many Buddha Yoga centers across the country so that anyone and everyone can practice yoga and apply Buddha's philosophy to upgrade and improve health, skills and prestige amongst everyone.

I am responsible towards Buddha, to the eternally dwelling Triple Gems and the Vietnamese Buddhism Sangha for the Buddha's philosophy that I am preaching to the community.

This is the way to perfect a person with health, wisdom (skill) and prestige, thereby building and developing the country. Anyone who lives by honesty and compassion, and works with a mind of sacrifice, patience and diligence is sure to succeed.

It was proved by the practical results of 45-year-long practice that with sacrifice, patience and diligence, one can create a career like the one I have today. After a very long time I practiced patiently. I shut myself up in a room for 7 years to practice Yogacara Vajrayana meditation. I studied in colleges for nine years and spent 18 years selling orchids in the market to complete the journey of sacrifice, patience, diligence, honesty and compassion.

After the process of practice and research, I found that people who want to apply the Buddha philosophy must have a three-dharma seal: Inner power, Mind power and Wisdom power.

You can gain Inner power by practicing yoga and meditation, mind power by practicing the Buddha philosophy, and Wisdom power by serving the community in real life with works and products. It leads to practical results. We must stand by ourselves on our feet and our own abilities. It was a route I made for myself.

In conclusion, the Institute of Vietnam Buddha Yoga Research and Application is for researching and applying the wisdom of the true mind to science, daily works and practicing methods for health. By following the five steps– sacrifice, patience, diligence, honesty and compassion– we are applying the Buddha philosophy without leaving the Buddha's path.

Today, the Institute of Vietnam Buddha Yoga Research and Application takes these five steps as a basis to convey Buddha's philosophy and yoga to the community and students of the institute in particular. Practice the non-worshiping, non-ritual and non-superstitious methods of Buddha Yoga to promote your own internal resources to benefit the community by 'Taking the true mind as your father, taking wisdom as your mother and taking the community as your family.' It is the criterion of a worthy human life to have great mind and great wisdom. In order to be like that, there must be a roadmap, which is the 5 aspects of the Buddha mind: Sacrifice, Patience, Diligence, Honesty and Compassion.

That is the route that we are following and guiding the community on.

This year, I am 81 years old but I still work continuously, preaching the Buddha philosophy to young people, and I do not want to stop. I taught at the Soc Son University for three years and the Van Hanh University for two years. I preached in Australia, Europe and the United States. I am looking for people to train, thereby introducing them to the path to achieve the Buddha wisdom.

III. THE OPERATING PRINCIPLES OF THE EIGHT CONSCIOUSSNESS OF HUMAN BEING

All the beings in this world, be they visible or invisible, or rough or subtle, have principles of their own operations. We can grasp the visible phenomena with our eyes, and by thinking about various operating principles, but for abstract and invisible phenomena, visions and thoughts are not sufficient grasp these principles. (It is also unlikely that the principles of true operation of objects with forms can be captured, so it is almost impossible to capture the operating principle of invisible phenomena). Because the eyesight of ordinary people is very limited, the phenomena can only be seen within a particular range, meanwhile, the thinking is involved by the ego, so we cannot see and capture the truth about the operating principle of the dharma.

From the micro particles suspended in air to the universe, there are always hidden principles of operations which allow them to co-exist with each other. And man is a miniature universe, consisting of two elements that constitute the Rupa (appearance) and the Dharma (also known as the five aggregates of the body-appearance, feeling, thought, action and consciousness). It constitutes the physical and psychological parts of being. They have a correlation. It is because of the physical part that the psychological part can have the knowing. The psychological part helps the physical part work efficiently. Physics and psychology are inseparable, which means that the body and mind are indissoluble; they rely on each other to exist in this world.

The operating principle of the human body as well as the whole universe can be grasped very well through common principles. It is the transformation of the four elements: earth, water, wind and fire (For the human body, the rigidity is called soil, the softness is called water, the fluidity is called wind, and the warmth is called fire), and the psychological part also has a very clear operating principle and always links with each other. This principle is the correlation of senses, causes and consciousness. The Rupa is the object of the senses: appearance is the object of the eye, sound is the object of the ear, smell is the object of the nose, taste is the object of the tongue, contact is the object of the body, and dharma (thoughts) is the object of the mind. After the six senses contact the six causes, the six consciousnesses appear. This is called the Eighteen Precepts.

And this operating principle follows the law of cause and effect. Because of sowing the seeds, we reap the fruits. We will get the results what we have sown. These causes will follow us through our reincarnation process and wait for conducive conditions to germinate and grow.

1. The unconscious reincarnation

If we attach ourselves to one of Eighteen Precepts, all Eighteen Precepts get infected. We cannot transform our consciousnesses into wisdom unless the passive process of reincarnation continues without any interruption. On the contrary, if we can convert one of the Eighteen Precepts to a pure precept, the eighteen precepts will be purified. If all the Eighteen Precepts are purified, we can transform the consciousnesses into wisdom and we will be proactive in the reincarnation.

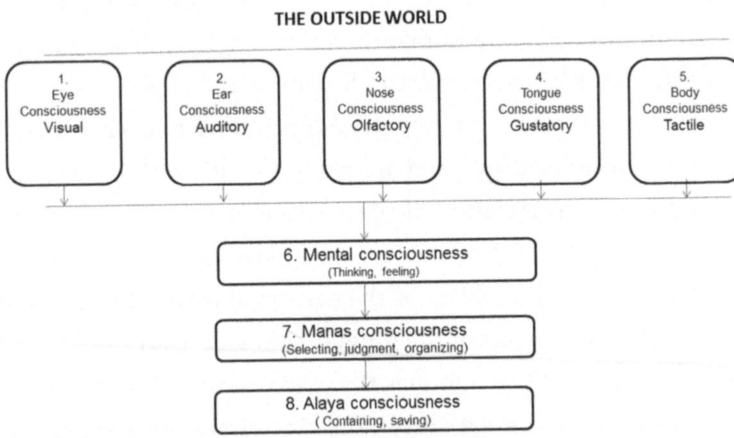

1. **The first Rupa is sight** - the object of the eye, which means that when the eye encounters the appearance of the object (color, shape and form), it then produces the awareness (consciousness) towards the desire or apathy of the color, or the shape and form of that object. Because of the ignorance obscured over countless lifetimes, wandering on the path of rebirth uncontrollably, we do not realize that it was a false scene. We start living the concept of discrimination (consciousness) that leads to the attachment (Manas Consciousness) into the subjective discrimination and starts a prerequisite process of uncontrolled reincarnation.

2. **The second Rupa is the sound** – the object of the ear, which means that when the ear encounters sound from the outer view, it immediately produces awareness (consciousness) towards a desire or apathy towards sound. Because of the ignorance obscured over countless lifetimes, wandering on the path of rebirth uncontrollably, we do not realize that it was a false scene. We start living the concept of discrimination (consciousness) towards sweet or acrid words, good or bad voices that lead to the attachment (Manas Consciousness) with subjective discrimination and start a prerequisite process of uncontrolled reincarnation.

3. **Third Rupa is the scent** – the object of the nose. It means that when the nose catches a scent from the outside, then it comes to know (consciousness) of desire. Because of the ignorance obscured from countless lifetimes, wandering on the path of rebirth uncontrollably, we do not realize that it was a false scene. We start the concept of discrimination (consciousness) of good or bad smell that leads to the attachment (Manas Consciousness) into the subjective discrimination and starts a prerequisite process of uncontrolled reincarnation.

4. **Fourth Rupa is the taste** – the object of the tongue, that is, when the tongue encounters the taste from the outer view, it then produces the knowing (the awakening) towards desire or apathy towards the taste. Because of the ignorance obscured over countless lifetimes, wandering on the path of rebirth uncontrollably, we do not realized that it is a false scene, but we initiate the distinction (consciousness) of good or bad taste, which leads to attachment (Manas Consciousness) into

subjective discrimination and starts a prerequisite process of uncontrolled reincarnation.

5. **Fifth Rupa is the feeling** - the object of the body is feeling, that is, when the body encounters a feeling from the external object, it then produces the knowing (consciousness) which in turn gives birth to a desire or apathy, or to criticize the feeling from that scene. Because of the ignorance obscured over countless lifetimes, wandering on the path of rebirth uncontrollably, we do not realize that it is a false scene, which initiates a distinction (consciousness) of soft, hard, hot, cold, dry or wet and leads to an attachment (Manas consciousness) to subjective discrimination and begins a prerequisite process of uncontrolled reincarnation.

6. **And final Rupa is dharma (thoughts)** - the object of the mind. This dharma has a vast meaning, showing the all things, phenomena, activities, concepts, as well as abstract problems, without form to exist, and of course also includes appearance, sounds, scents, flavors and sensations. It is the brain which is able to handle the input information that the senses put receive, compare it with data stored in the memory (Alaya or the eighth consciousness) to gain awareness. So, when the mind is exposed to the outside contexts, it will create a discrimination in the mind, called consciousness. Because of this discrimination, it comes to attachment (Manas consciousness), to subjective discrimination, and a prerequisite process of uncontrolled reincarnation.

7. **The essence of the five senses** is to gather information

from scenes that create the consciousness of appearance, sound, scent, taste, and feeling. After that, the process of awareness (thinking, judging and comparing) begins where all the information from the knowledge of the five senses bring the discrimination. When the information is processing, if we re awake and aware of it, then wisdom will appear. However, in case of the absence of the knowledge of things, this phenomenon is analyzed by the interference of consciousness, the distinction of color, sound, scent, taste, and feeling and will be stored in Alaya consciousness again through an attachment consciousness (Manas), and what is saved in this will be the cause of the uncontrolled rebirth process.

Alaya consciousness is compared with the ocean. On the surface of the ocean, there are waves and swirls, but deep down, it is quiet and pure. The cause of the presence of waves and swirls is the wind. Because of the wind, the ocean can create the waves.

The wave is the affliction, and the cause of the affliction is the wind (discrimination and attachment). Waves are a phenomenon, and the ocean is the nature. The waves that are created by the ocean finally merge to the ocean. So, in a vast ocean, the phenomenon of waves and swirls can only shock the surface of the ocean, so that in the depths of the ocean it remains quiet, clear and pure. Afflictions cannot touch the True Mind. The True Mind is in the depths of the ocean, while the afflictions are on the surface. If we want to go deep down, we must let go of discrimination and attachment. Because we cannot let go of these, we cannot bring it to peace, and we will be beaten by the waves of affliction. It is impossible to return to the True Mind, which means that we continue to be forced by karma, thereby being led to an unconscious rebirth.

The root of the attachment comes from the delusion and attachment to the distinction of ego (I and myself). You become so greedy to hold onto it as though it's yours and if anyone touches it, anger rises in your mind. There are three poisons – greed, hate and ignorance– which are the root cause of unconscious rebirth.

We can have the distinctive consciousness of knowing that there is the right and wrong, visible and invisible, True self and Ego, good and bad, on the condition that the consciousness is purified (fully awaken and awareness). It means you have discrimination without attachment, as if this distinction would not create conscious karma. If your consciousness is not purified, then that distinction will create conscious karma which will pull you away.

Whether the person who has obtained the dharma, Buddhas or Bodhisattvas has discrimination or not, the discrimination of these transcendent ones is no longer containing selfishness and greed. They are already enlightened. On the contrary, the distinction of human beings is full of affliction, confusion and suffering.

We are here because in the past, we have been afraid of the string of afflictions and impure causes that were stored in the consciousness. Our consciousness still exists after we die. It has a duty to lead us to rebirth. Depending on the heavy or light karma that we have created, we are reborn respectively in the realm of Heaven, Human beings, Atula, Preta or Hell. Therefore, in a new regeneration environment and new body, the impure seeds are kept in the mind, not only undamaged, but also very healthy and always waiting to be eligible conditions for germination, root growth and development.

Because they are impure seed of the past, they are now going to draw us away; we will be dominated by them. We cannot see the 'clear light'. The seeds of conscious karma in consciousness will grow, and this growth process will be manifested through the attachment of consciousness, and this attachment will lead to the discrimination of eye, ear, nose, tongue and body which are the effects we have to bear. These five impure consciousnesses will create more impure seeds which are saved in the Alaya consciousness. These five impure consciousnesses will lead to the discrimination of consciousness, and the impure consciousness will lead to an attachment and the new seed of karma will be saved in Alaya to carry on to a new non- continuous reincarnation.

2. Master the reincarnation

The principle of mastering the reincarnation is similar to the unconscious reincarnation. It is also under the law of cause and effect from the past to the present. We all exist due to the practices that prevailed in the past, where there was the attachment and discrimination that led to the impurity of the first five consciousnesses. This process and rebirth are the same. But, in a controlled rebirth, there is a new process from the impurity of the five consciousnesses.

For the impurity of these five consciousnesses, we have a practice where we turn the distinction of consciousness into observation of the mind, proceeding to the transformation the Manas consciousness which is to equal wisdom and the Alaya consciousness to the Great Wisdom Mirror. When these three consciousnesses are transformed into wisdom, the five consciousnesses will be purified and will turn into enlightened wisdom (also called practical wisdom), which is the last to be transmitted by the previous three consciousnesses.

When the consciousnesses have been transformed into wisdom, we are no longer bound by karma. So, after death, we will master our own rebirth and we will be completely free from cycle of birth and death.

3. The path of transforming the consciousnesses to wisdom

During our existence in this life, if we master ourselves by mastering our own thoughts, we will master rebirth, because if we master our thoughts while we are alive, we can also master ourselves at the time of death. Where we want to be reborn is based on our honesty and compassion. Our karma is no longer leading us as we are awakened, aware, intuitive and enlightened towards and the illusions of desires and outside scenes can be cleverly defended and controlled by the consciousnesses. This freedom requires a path-the path to change consciousness to wisdom. If we can transform the consciousness to wisdom, we can break the elimination of ignorance and find our own True Mind.

The path of turning the consciousness to the Wisdom of Observing, Manas Consciousness to the Wisdom of Equality,

Alaya Consciousness into the Great Wisdom of Mirror and the five consciousnesses of senses to the Enlightened Application Wisdom is the path of applying the mind of sacrifice, patience and diligence from which there is a life full of honesty and compassion.

I have practiced and experienced this path. It is very practical and not abstract. We just need to have faith and try our best to go. Living life has a sacrifice mind to break the distinction, because when there is sacrifice, there is no self, and when there is no self, there is naturally no discrimination. And it is from here the notion of discrimination and attachment no longer exists.

If we have no discrimination, our consciousness of the outside scenes will be there but because of the way we are processing the information, it does not affect us and it comes to our Alaya consciousness with pure seeds. Then, if the seed come to the knowing, it is the pure knowing, it is the wisdom knowing.

Therefore, using the mind of sacrifice, we will gain the Wisdom of Observation. We must live a life of patience in order to be able to free ourselves from predestined adversities, so that we can break the attachment, because when we come to a predestined adversity having no patience, we will attach ourselves to it, which is very painful. For the advantage of money, lust, fame, food and sleep, we also need to have patience, because without patience, we will follow it, be bound by it and will be unable to walk on the road to salvation. Using the mind of patience, we will achieve Wisdom of Equality. We have to live a life of diligence; this diligence is the source of energy to promote sacrifices and patience, which are always actively trying to transform bad seeds in Alaya. If so, using this mind, we will achieve the Wisdom of Great Mirror.

Accordingly, the five senses consciousnesses will turn to the Wisdom of Enlightened Application. Because their nature is the senses of human form, they are like a lens of camera used to collect information from the scene, and their perception is due to the mind, so we cannot transform them. If you change, you must transform from the mind, the mind is pure, of course, the image will also be pure, and for this reason the first five are the final ones of transforming into wisdom.

When practicing and experiencing these three minds, the life with honesty and compassion will surely exist. Honesty and compassion are the Emptiness and Compassion. When you can transform consciousnesses to wisdom, of course, also synonymous with seeing the true nature of the dharmas is the emptiness. Emptiness does not mean nothing. It is all due to the conditions that are combined to manifest into forms. If all the conditions are gone, all the forms will be back to emptiness and there will be no birth or death; there will be no cause and effect and all will be non-duality. Once we can see with this Vajrayana's vision, we can join real life and experience success. And when we achieve emptiness (Sunyata Prajna wisdom), then the real compassion arises hence giving rise to the compassion for community, 'Taking the mind to be a father, taking the wisdom to be a mother, taking the community to become family.'

4. There is a way, do not neglect

For the practice of Tantrayana, the transformation of the practitioner's mind is of paramount importance, because the mind leads the forms, but the forms cannot lead the mind. Every miserable thing is caused by the mind, and the enlightenment or immersion in delusion also comes from the mind. So, it is necessary to transform your own mind to have your own honesty, to have your own compassion, and to avoid falling into the realm of suffering.

On the path of transforming the consciousness into wisdom, as I have analyzed, we must try to practice it according to that path to have true joy in this life. Remember, the way we go going to hell or Nirvana is our decision. Be wise to create an ideal and a goal for you. We are young, have to sacrifice our youth, patience with ups and downs, diligently go on a difficult road, not forget the original mind, live together with honesty and compassion, then we will have achievements on the way of practicing and application.

Don't be too concerned about the outside scene, because they are illusory scenes and will melt like dew in the early sunshine. So, don't discriminate to distort and attach on to the outside scenes, but let it be natural.

When the consciousnesses of the five senses realize the presence of appearance, sound, flavor, taste and feeling, and then let this knowing stop and watch it, and don't let the discrimination of consciousness come in and lose the purity of mind. Know and stop, and be 'heartless' towards it. If we know, but we are not attaching to our knowing, we can separate the distinction of consciousness, and when we leave the discrimination of consciousness, we will return to our own pure mind. The Surangama Samadhi sutra says: *knowing and leaving the knowing is the way to Nirvana, knowing and attach to the is the way to hell.*

Therefore, we must transform our consciousness to be pure and to be aware of the purity, then we will be like the awakening of the Manas consciousness and will stop judging. Then the knowing from consciousness will go directly to the Alaya consciousness, but these stored seeds are pure seeds. Because they are pure seeds, when we confront the rebirth, we will keep the initiative, we will not be bound by karma.

When our mind is affected by the external scenes, the Alaya consciousness will bring out the appearance, sounds, scents, flavors and sensations. They will pull us away if we are not awake. Just like when we accidentally heard a song that we have heard in the past, if we don't have the awareness – the missing and feeling about the context– the desire will rise and lead us to finding the old street or ex-lover thereby making us lose our wisdom. If we are awake and are aware of those things because of the seeds in Alaya consciousness, then we can observe our thoughts and face them with a big smile. This smile is very natural, having such naturalness that we can see the true nature of the dharma is empty, returning to emptiness, returning to ourselves, living in our own peacefulness and happiness and not needing lean on anyone. It is living with yourself, alone but not lonely; the soul is full of joy.

The sight of the eyes, the hearing of the ears, the smell of the nose, the taste of the tongue and the collision of the body, we have the right to use it all but not to be attached to the sensory objects. Let us see them as a skillful means, that is to live with the temptations of life that we are not infected with. We transform these temptations into a means for us to achieve wisdom. When there is wisdom, we apply it with honesty and compassion. So, if there is a way, you must be diligent. Do not neglect diligence because of some difficulty and a little desire for yourself. Overcome it, turn it to the skillful means and we will have a great achievement for arising wisdom.

IV. THE PRIMITIVE PURE MIND OF HUMAN BEING

1. Sakyamuni Buddha discovered Buddhahood

The theory and application of the Buddha philosophy system can be traced back more than 2500 years ago, to the time of Sakyamuni Buddha. Sakyamuni Buddha, to distinguish himself from other enlightened beings (Buddhas) who appeared before or after him, was born a prince of the name of Siddhartha in the sixth century BC. According to the legend of Buddha, in the first 29 years of his life, he was almost imprisoned in the joyous castles built by his father, king Śuddhodana. Finally, when he was exposed to old age, sickness and death, he escaped the royal palace and went on the way to end all grievances of discontent.

For six years, he practiced intense asceticism, trying to attain mindfulness and to master his mind. He found that it was wrong to force him from extreme joy to extreme austerity. Finally, he followed the middle way, without any greed for passion or austerity avoiding all other extremes. He was able to clear the most miserable suffering and ignorance from his mind and become a fully awakened and wise person- a Buddha. In the remaining 49 years of his life, he taught the method of the middle way in lifestyle and in practice with many different ways, keeping up with the personality and ability of each person.

Buddha's philosophy is what keeps us from suffering and the cause of suffering. It contains thousands of different ways to overcome the obstacles of mind and body that make us unhappy. The deepest foundation of this philosophy is our pure True Mind or Buddhahood.

2. The original purity of the Buddhahood

According to Buddha's philosophy, no matter how much confusion we can be in in the present, our essential and pure nature remains pure and tranquil. Just as clouds can temporarily obscure the sun but cannot affect the sun's ability to shine, likewise, the grief of body and mind in the period - such as anxiety, confusion and anxiety the misery it causes - can only temporarily obscure but cannot destroy or even affect the basic purity of our mind. Deeply in our hearts as well as all sentient beings, we are in the endless source of compassion and wisdom. The ultimate goal of every dharma practice whether it is Buddhist or not, is to reveal that essence, in contact with that pure nature.

When we have developed clarity in ourselves, compassion, selflessness and compassion within us, we can see the clarity and compassion reflects on us. When we have not been able to touch those qualities in ourselves, we will see everyone have evil and narrow mind. Because whatever we see from outside is only the reflection of reality in our minds.

The presence of pure nature is not a matter of closing your eyes to believing or accepting a dogma, but an empirical fact. Countless people in the past have discovered that great treasure in the mind, the treasure of peace, compassion and wisdom. How many great masters have said that we can discover our own profound nature to be of immense bliss that is bought by nature? Buddha is such a loving master, and all his doctrine and methods that is the key to help us reach that potential supreme of human being.

In the term of Buddhist philosophy, the ultimate purpose of human evolution is enlightenment. This shows when all the enchanters go on ignorance and what obscures the mind is eradicated, and when all goodness in us is fully developed. That perfect accomplishment, that full awakening is characterized by infinite wisdom, infinite compassion and immense capacity or means.

3. The methods of transforming awareness

In the direction of awakening transformation, the path to achieve wisdom is a sequential process of purifying the mind from mistakes and limitations, instead, promoting virtues such as wisdom and compassion. This path includes creating special factors such as keeping your own pure mind, developing concentration and wisdom training, etc. so that the future will achieve full awareness. It is because of the emphasis on factor creation for a future outcome, but the gradual approach is sometimes called "humanity" (meaning the cause) to lead to the practical application of wisdom.

Those who practice the awakening, transformation method can take the future consequences of spiritual practice as the starting point of practice. In other words, the practitioner of this method will think, speak and act it right at the present as if they were a Buddha.

According to the awakening transformation method, the integrity is not waiting for us at a future time in the way of thinking: "If we now practice seriously, our future will become a Buddha" or "If we have morality in this world, we will go to heaven in the next life." In this way, heaven is now: we should be a Buddha right at the present; but we are caught up in the limited concepts like men are like this, women are like that, we were born that way it can't be different, etc. That's why we have inner conflicts and conflicts with others. All these conflicts will vanish if we practice Vajrayana, which means realizing the fact that every man or woman is fully self-sufficient. Moreover, every man and woman contain both yin and yang abilities. The reality is that each of us is a union of all cosmic capacities. All we need to be integrity is already in us right now, only that we are able to realize it or not.

4. The transforming principles

The core of the universe and all living things is non-stop movement and transformation. As modern science proves, the physical universe with so many nuances, from the smallest molecule to the largest nebula, is just a state that constantly transforms and evolves from one form of energy to another other quantities. Our body and mind are also energy: we are healthy or sick; our mind is stable or unstable, depending on whether the physical energy of our mind is in harmony. By practicing this method properly, all of our energy, including the very intense but subtle energies that we are often unaware of, is used to achieve the most important transformation. In every transformation, it is from a human being who is passionate, confused and limited in the shell of the ego to become a fully awake, aware person (aware and mastering every thoughts and actions), have a loving and wise awareness.

How do we do such an extraordinary transformation? Where to find the necessary materials to bring such a profound change? We do not need to look far away. It is not necessary to withdraw that energy from the atomic nucleus, or to use the spacecraft to launch into space to find that energy in a distant planet. In fact, the core energy to make that profound transformation is the energy of our own desires.

V. APPLY SACRIFICE, PATIENCE, DILIGENCE, HONESTY AND COMPASSION TO TRANSFORM THE EIGHT CONSCIOUSNESS TO WISDOM

His Holiness Vasubandhu took the philosophy of Lankavatara Sutra and Samdhinirmocana Sutra of Buddha to create the

Vijnanaptivàda sutra, it is the sutra of transforming eight consciousnesses of human being to Buddha wisdoms. The key of Buddha sutra is about leaving the attachment and discrimination in our mind to get into the Tathagata or the Buddhahood. Then we will achieve the Buddha wisdoms.

The Lankavatara philosophy was taught by Buddha. The Vasubandhu took this philosophy to develop into the method of transforming the consciousness to wisdom. To know how to turn consciousness into wisdom, we must grasp the principle of operation of the consciousness system as follows:

Our cognitive process must undergo eight consciousnesses, of which the first six ones are eyes, ears, nose, tongue, body and mind. The knowing discrimination of the mind helps us see colors and distinguish everything. After that, the perceptions of the five sense faculties are acquired by the sixth consciousness. Then, they are transferred to the seventh consciousness, from which these insights are sent to the eighth consciousness, which stores all that the five senses faculties perceived through the reception process of the sixth and seventh consciousness. This process takes place continuously and creates karma seeds in the eighth consciousness. All of these five receptors are indistinguishable. The information is judged by the sixth consciousness whether to attach or not (thinking and feeling), and the seventh consciousness adds in the discrimination which is then saved in the eighth consciousness which is like the CPU of a computer.

If a situation similar to one that is 30 years old and has been stored in the consciousness is encountered again, the old knowledge will change to the seventh consciousness that distinguishes between the good and the bad, causing us to create karma. The first five consciousnesses are called the cognitive consciousnesses, and are five perceived senses, which include eyes, ears, nose, tongue and body. The cognitive part is the nervous system that leads these five bases into Alaya consciousness. These five consciousnesses are external perceptions which are incapable of distinguishing morals, so they belong to the neutral consciousness (unaffected by subjective perceptions). The sixth consciousness is subjective and distinguishes awareness, the seventh consciousness is attached consciousness and he eighth consciousness is contained consciousness.

The sixth consciousness is the present knowledge and perception. This consciousness is a compilation of information from the five previous senses from 'seeing' the external phenomenal world. It distinguishes right from left, black from white, cold from hot, and specializes in self-criticizing, distinguishing, calculating and measuring the basis of the information that has been brought by the previous senses. This consciousness creates karma due to discrimination, speculation and the decision leading to manifesting specific actions by body, words or thoughts, or by love-hate desire. The sixth consciousness is Ideation, our conscious thought, referred to in Buddhist thought as the Monkey Mind, because it is typically unsettled and constantly chattering with what we have known as emotion.

If we know how to use the mind to sacrifice all thoughts that arise in our mind, then the six consciousnesses are transformed into the wisdom of discernment.

For example: When we apply our mind to sacrifice in work, we do not distinguish the time and space, and we do not calculate the gain and loss. We totally focus on finishing the work without fatigue and thoughts of affliction. We scarify the mind of calculating time and space, benefit, laziness, greed, sadness or happiness. It is the mind of sacrifice. We can accomplish everything if we sacrifice the narrow mind, the attachment to time and space, and the lazy mind, then, at that time, wisdom of discernment appears. Observing the mind helps us to see things outside phenomena as it is and not distorted and unobstructed.

The seventh consciousness obscures the human nature by ego and the attachment to ego. It is the place to store and gather the existence of the unreal outer world, turning them into seeds of illusion, from which it is said that there is a particular inner self that pollutes the information of the previous six consciousnesses. This seventh consciousness also pollutes the eighth consciousness by continuously giving the eighth consciousness a thought that exists in space and time.

The perception of this seventh consciousness is wrong because of its attaching nature that creates four types of illusions: Self-centered belief, Self-centered compassion, Self-centered delusion, and Self-centered esteem.

The nature of Manas consciousness is ignorance, discrimination and attachment. It is imprisoned in the desire to exist forever and always desires to satisfy sexual desires. The natural operation of the seventh consciousness is to seek sensuality. It pushes us toward sensual pleasure, but because this consciousness is obstructed, it does not know where we are going. It thinks that it seeks happiness but actually results in more suffering than happiness.

Usually, the signs of our seventh consciousness that manifests outwardly are our attachment, stubbornness, quarrelsome, refusing to listen, always thinking that we are good, not accepting our faults, like expressing our egos.

If we use the mind of patience to break that attachment, we turn this consciousness into equality of mind. For example, when someone says bad things about us, if we can smile happily, not annoyed, it means that we are applying patience. When we listen to other people, we quietly listen to what they have to say but our heart doesn't start attachment and distinguish it. It means we have successfully applied patience.

Sakyamuni Buddha practiced patience with a begging bowl for 49 years. Now, we can practice patience in life and work.

When our mind is patient, and in a state where attachment does not occur, then the seventh consciousness is said to be pure and the equality of mind occurs. Equality of mind gives us a true perception that we are someone who perceives the truth that all beings and phenomena are essentially equal without any discrimination. There is no self, no hate or compassion, no taking or leaving, no near or far, no deep or shallow, no clean or dirty, no more or less, and so on.The main part of our consciousness is the eighth consciousness, the Alaya consciousness (containing, storing) and the basis for the other seven consciousnesses. Alaya is also known as 'contains all images' (treasure). It is from this place again that all the concepts of the self (ego) and its operating behaviors in the external world (attachment) arise. If we can illustrate this consciousness as an immense sea, the other seven are the undulating or rushing waves on that surface. Accordingly, the previous seven consciousness cannot be separated from this eighth consciousness, nor can the tranquility in the depths of the sea be disturbed; water and waves are one, so, these eight consciousnesses are fundamentally one. We also find this example of water and waves in the doctrine of Sunyata (emptiness).

This eighth consciousness is transcending. It has no intention in its operation, does not recognize the object, does not distinguish, and is not obscured, neither good or bad and is always in a state of stillness.

Alaya consciousness is a place to store seeds due to the act of creation starting from the cause to the result (karma) due to our delusional actions. This consciousness does not create karma, but it acts as the subject of karmic retribution for deliberate actions of the past, resulting in the present, and influences the activities and attachments to the future. It leads us to reincarnate in the three realms (trayo dhātava) and the nine lands. The ripening process of the seeds, the thoughts and the perceptions of the objects are all subjective; so that process and its results are not real.

The liberation from the cycle of reincarnation is when all the seeds of afflictions are replaced by pure seeds, created by pure karma. Alaya consciousness also contains pure intrinsic seeds, which are the source and will guide us towards enlightenment. When enlightenment is attained, this eighth consciousness has no immature seeds (anomaly) anymore, and transforms into the Mirror-like wisdom.

Alaya consciousness has two parts- The subject part and the perceived object part. The first part is interdependent with the seventh consciousness, while the second part is predestined with the sixth and fifth consciousnesses which express through the states of intellect, morality and spirituality, such as desire, calculation, analysis, meditation, trust, shame, wisdom, etc. When the second part is changed during enlightenment, it becomes posterior wisdom. Although Alaya is predestined with all three types of transformation to transform consciousness into wisdom, but within it, it also has a permanent basis that maintains the ideals of purity, immutability and permanence.

When the sixth and seventh consciousnesses are transferred, the eighth consciousness is transformed into the Mirror-like wisdom. At this point, it is automatically transferred to the Mirror-like wisdom because at this time the eighth consciousness is pure and can be transferred to the Tathagata or true mind.

In short, humans have two qualities, intellect and wisdom. Intellectuals like to distinguish attachment and wisdom is the understanding and application in all things without discrimination and attachment. Then, there is no consciousness karma that is contained in our eighth consciousness; there is no resentment, so it is called liberation.

The mind of discrimination is due to ignorance. So, in order to leave the discriminating mind and transform it into a non-discriminating mind or to wisdom of discernment, there must be a mind of sacrifice. If you want to return to the wisdom of equality, thereby freeing yourself of your attachments, you must exercise patience. Then, we apply these two minds diligently in order to leave the mind discrimination and attachment and gain the Buddha wisdom.

So, in order to have a skill or wisdom, the practitioner must practice the three Buddha rituals- sacrifices, patience and diligence.

The five sense consciousnesses transform into the all-accomplishing wisdom.

VI. AWAKENING - AWARENESS - INTUITION - ENLIGHTMENT

The Buddha philosophy and its application, both comes from the true mind. Therefore, the person who practices the Buddha philosophy needs to take the True mind to be the basis for his practice.

This philosophy shows us how to apply the wisdom of true mind. The practitioner needs to realize that the true mind has been inside him from the very beginning of his life. This pure mind, also known as Buddhahood, does not disappear, but because of ignorance, we do not realize it. The Buddhas of the three lives that appear in this world are also for the sole purpose of showing us the pure mind and apply it to life for peace and happiness.

So, how can we transform using consciousness to wisdom? How can we get rid of suffering and unhappiness to bring permanent peace and happiness in our life?

There are four steps to enlightenment- awakening, awareness, intuition and enlightenment.

How to be awakened?

How to be aware?

How to be intuitive?

How to be enlightened?

All methods do not leave this key. It is including everything. Everyone has it, and everyone can achieve it but not many people can apply it. If a person realizes it, he will be enlightened.

How do we apply this wisdom?

We must apply the wisdom of True Mind according to the following four precepts:

1. Do not give up the True Mind.
2. Do not leave your Bodhi mind - the honest and compassionate mind.
3. Do not hide your wisdom; teach new generations and share your knowledge with the community.
4. Do not do things that are not beneficial to the community.

According to the Mahayana spirit, Buddha is the True mind, and only when a person is enlightened can he apply this miraculous wisdom of the true mind.

It can be said that the most important thing of the Buddha philosophy to open the wisdom of true mind and then apply it. When we face adversity, a thought arises to destroy all difficulties.

The Buddha philosophy is a philosophy of natural science and practical results in human life. It is not a doctrine for research and discussion. The Buddha philosophy is a practical experience, going into life in a normal and natural way. The philosophy of Buddha helps people to overcome themselves, to lead a fulfilling life that you can see the silence in yourself and the soul that is not disturbed by anxious lust and fear. Therefore, you will have a natural, innocent and fearless life in the middle of this lively and colorful life.

Awakening, awareness, intuition and enlightenment are the intellectual steps of Buddha wisdom.

Awakening is the moment you know the thoughts that arise in your mind but do not let the illusions of consciousness disturbing your thinking. Awareness is the constant application of the unbroken knowing. Intuition is the application of permanent awareness immediately with the non-discriminatory mind. Enlightenment is the silent mind where no thoughts arise, but you know everything.

We apply five these minds of sacrifice, patience, diligence, honesty and compassion to achieve awakening, awareness, intuition and enlighten stages.

Why can these rituals do that?

We humans have two qualities, intellect and wisdom. Intellect is the acquisition, synthesis and the cultivation of knowledge from the outside. Wisdom is emitting from within each person. It is the capacity of each human being.

We are conducting business and scientific research, and applying science in our work and daily lives. What are we applying, intellect or wisdom? Does each of us ever ask ourselves what we are here for?

I have set up a roadmap of awakening, awareness, intuition, and enlightenment to train students. It is always to be able to control the conceptual thoughts which are the consciousness operating in our mind. If we control right at the moment our thought arises, we can convert the selfish, greedy and jealous thoughts into the thoughts that can benefit the community.

It is using the awakening to transforming consciousness to wisdom and applies the intuition.

It means that we transform illusion, discrimination, and greed to the path of awakening, awareness, intuition and enlightenment. This is a parallel route, taking the path of awakening, awareness, intuition and enlightenment to transform the discrimination knowledge into wisdom.

We transform the eight senses eyes, ears, nose, tongue, body, mind, Manas and Alaya into four wisdoms, all-accomplishing wisdom, wisdom of discernment, wisdom of equality and mirror-like wisdom. When you can achieve the Buddha wisdom and apply it into life, you have the fifth Buddha wisdom.

We take the path of wisdom to fix the mind of greed, selfishness and discrimination to the great, equal and compassionate mind.

We use the mind of sacrifices to leave the greedy and selfish mind. The mind of patience is to correct the discriminating mind.

The mind of diligence is to correct the lazy mind. We build up our credibility by being honest and loving. Thus, when you know how to use these mind rituals to rectify your life, your life will be free and peaceful.

I have taken these five minds as the basis of Tantricism, taking the application as a path of practice for tantric practitioners. A person who has this foundation goes out into the society, in any environment, any situation, any company, any family, or any community he will also need it. Thus, it can be said that this is the most important human property.

We have to have self-realization and fix it ourselves. We should not receive or depend on other people for our own freedom. If we encounter difficult times or ups and downs in life, we must take it as a chance to practice these five minds to cultivate wisdom. This is the path of my life that I have been on from the past to the accomplishing day.

You must take the five rituals of the Buddha's mind to proceed in your life in the right direction, and no longer a wandering mind. If you obtain the five minds of Buddha, you enter life to enlighten your inner wisdom.

We have wandered too long in samsara, coming and going aimlessly. Our mind is often wandering without a clear path to go on to enlighten our wisdom. So, we do not have the lucid willpower, and are always hindered and bound by the narrow mind and ego because we do not have enough inner power, mental power and wisdom power.

The mind of sacrifice, patience, diligence, honesty and compassion is also the faculty of Buddhahood.

Awakening, awareness, intuition and enlightenment is the wisdom of Buddhahood.

More than 2500 years ago, Shakyamuni also began his journey of practice of the five rituals - sacrifice, patience, diligence, honesty and compassion. The five years of searching for the truth, 6 years of asceticism and 49 years of bringing a bowl to beg for alms, were just to train his mind and practice his wisdom. He took difficulties to train his mind and to eliminate his own ego.

The first sentence, 'Hardships are the successful steps of the wises one and the abyss of the coward and lazy.' I write this sentence to remind us that on our path, we should never give up in the middle of the way. When you meet the suffering time, if you know how to apply the mind of sacrifice, patience and diligence to overcome it, you will succeed.

The second sentence, 'It is hard to find honest people / It is more difficult to bring people back to the truth / A dishonest life is a meaningless life / The dishonest work is unethical work / A person who is dishonest with himself is not honest with anyone.' It is to remind us that we must always live with honestly and compassion. If you want to have peaceful and happy life, never deceive yourself or other people, it not, you will get the bad sequences corresponding to the law of cause and effect. If you treat others with honesty and compassion, you will help create a community with positive energy around you, without the resentment of suffering, and you will have good prestige as well.

1. Use the mind of sacrifice to enter the awakening stage

When we apply the mind to sacrifice to leave our narrow mind and selfish ego, the Bodhi mind naturally arises. At that time, we do everything not with devotion of our ego, but for the benefit of the community.

In order to apply the mind of self-sacrifice, practitioners must always be mindful. The mindfulness always controls each of its own thoughts. We will look into the nature of each thought. Is it that through come from the discrimination and attachment? When we are recognizing each thought clearly, we apply the mind of self-sacrifice to leave the mind of selfishness, narrowness and our attachment to fame, money and sex.

We are aware of every action and every work to see if we have any selfishness or jealousy for taking advantage of ourselves? If you see, then you use the mind to sacrifice to let go the attachment with these thoughts.

If people are selfish, what will happen? They will sell fake and low quality products. They may win once, twice or thrice, but, in the end, people will know and they will lose credit and they will eliminate themselves. Just like the suffering of humans due to eating food that is fertilized with toxic chemicals where they accumulated the toxins for a long time and it makes them sick that they have to see doctor. If the doctor does not have a good heart, he makes the patients suffer more. Then they go to the drug store or the pharmacist who sells them fake drugs or drugs at a high price because he has to spend a lot of money for marketing.

They are now suffering even more. Those who participate in that chain think they are serving people, but if with a selfish mind, they create misery for people.

From this example, we must always review our work to see if we are causing suffering for us and for others? Also, each thought that leads to an action must be controlled. Is it from the pure honest mind to the community or the selfish greedy mind? We must consider finding the truth of our motivation.

The person who applies the wisdom must always control these thoughts as it has four stages– awakening, awareness, intuition and enlightenment. We must always return to ourselves, and see and accept our fault. Since, it is then that we know how to correct our mistake. Then, wisdom will appear.

Thus, we must apply the mind of sacrifice to abandon the mind of desire, selfishness, greed, jealousy and pride in order to have a great and pure mind. From there, we do everything for the benefit of the community. If we can do so, we achieve the wisdom of discernment.

When we are constantly awakened to control our own thoughts, then we know how to apply the self-sacrificing mind to let go of all selfishness, patiently overcoming all difficulties and challenges. We will know how to live in harmony with life, do what needs to be done, not go against the nature and believe in ourselves. We should always return to our own power, not seek strength from outside sources or be slaves to anything, even meditation or Buddhas.

Each thought arises in the mind; we have to control to see if what we say will bring negativity to people?

We have to promote our own internal strength. If we can promote our own experiences and skills without praying for help from anyone, we will make our life full.

However, we must not be proud of our limited knowledge. If we only use our voice and communication skills to direct others, and refuse to put our effort and energy into work, how can we have an honest and equal mind. How can we feel peace and happiness? Even though there is wisdom, it must be devoted for the benefit of the community, so that the wisdom of equality can appear.

Thus, practitioners constantly control each of their own thoughts by being awake and aware, and always apply the five rituals of sacrifices, patience, diligence, honesty and compassion. If you can do that, you will keep your body, mouth, and mind pure and avoid mistakes.

2. Use the mind of patience to enter awareness

If we don't have patience, we won't succeed. If you are patient, you can bring peace and happiness to others. On the contrary, if there is no patience, there is no success.

We must exercise patience when we face adversities in life. When people bring difficulties to us, we exercise patience so that we do not angry or attach to the feeling that we see as a challenge that we have to overcome. Because all difficulties are the means for us to attain wisdom and train our mind power- the wisdom power.

The person who creates adversity is a teacher who trains us to be patient, scarified. Adversity is the means to bringing ourselves to wisdom and success.

How can we overcome ourselves and help others achieve success if we do not exercise a patient mind?

If we learn something, but do not have enough patience to practice it and apply it in our life, we cannot promote our own wisdom and skills. We have to set up a path to practice; we cannot sit there and enjoy it. If we just study and keep the knowledge to ourselves, we move farther away from wisdom.

We do not say that we are patient, but we apply patience to overcome all the challenges in life. When all the adversities come and we always apply this patient mind, our mind returns to the wisdom of equality and achieves the pure mind.

Do not misunderstand that patience is disadvantageous, in fact, it is the opposite. The disadvantage is only temporary, but the mind and blessing of the patient one will endure, increase and will be rewarded with good consequences. It is like water and fertilizer for the road to go to the blooming of wisdom flower, happiness and peace in life.

The application of patience is like wearing solemn armor for us. It is a shining example to achieve wisdom. Because of the application of the patient mind, the mind is pure and wisdom power is rising.

The person who exercises patience will know what he should do in right time and right place. If he does not know what to do at the right time and place, he will patently wait for it. It is the patent wisdom of the Buddha mind.

Thus, overcoming all circumstances are those who have successfully applied patience.

3. Use your diligent mind to enter your intuition

Diligence is everything to do with focus, steadfastness and effort until the result is achieved. Despite difficulties, we are not discouraged or lazy and do not give up in the middle of the way. We are constantly contemplating the error in our body and mind due to our laziness. It is the application of the diligent mind.

Because of the diligent mind, the practitioner can gain a successful career. If we do not practice having a diligent mind, we cannot do anything and no one will appreciate us. In all karma of body and mind, laziness is the greatest karma. For example, when you are practicing meditation but you feel pain and sleepy, you must use the diligent mind to subdue that lazy mind. Whatever you do, don't ever quit. The diligent mind is used to conquer lazy thoughts and ego.

If we constantly apply the diligent mind, it will give us a tough endurance to forget tirelessly to the wisdom to achieve our career.

Thus, the diligent mind applicator is one who has a firm belief in his own true mind and his wisdom mind is like a burning fire.

4. Applying meditation to go on the way to awakening, awareness, intuition and enlightenment

Prajna Paramita meditation is a mindfulness of constantly controlling one's own arising thoughts to leave the mind of distraction, discrimination and outward thoughts.

Thus, the application of the mind of sacrifice, patience and diligence is in order to leave the attachment and discrimination to attain a pure and lucid mind. If the mind is clear, your working is neatly, accurately and quickly done for the benefit of oneself and for others. It means you are working in the meditating stage.

5. Achieve Fundamental wisdom

If you can apply the five rituals- sacrifice, patience, diligence, honesty and compassion, your consciousness will be transformed into wisdom and the pure mind will appear. The Paramita wisdom cannot use words to express it all because this is the wisdom of the pure mind that is applied to life, stays in fame and fortune without getting caught in it, and often brings its benefits to oneself and community. We always apply the five minds to all situations and thoughts without being discerned and attached by the illusion mind so that we will be always pure, honest and compassionate.

Conclusion: The roadmap of applying the five rituals of sacrifice, patience, diligence and honesty and compassion to transform knowledge into mind as I have shown above is:

The mind of sacrifice transforms the sixth consciousness into wisdom of discernment.

The mind of patience transforms the seventh consciousness - the discrimination and attachment to the wisdom of equality.

The mind of diligence transforms the eighth consciousness into mirror-like wisdom.

I practiced these minds in my 45 years of meditation, 19 years of entering into life to grow orchids, to managing 2 companies, Thanh Quang Orchids Ltd and Vietnam Ngoc Linh Ginseng joint stock company, institute of Vietnam Buddha yoga research and application. I applied the Five Mahayana Buddhism to my dharma realm to train my students in these five rituals through work and daily life. As a result, I have good health, skills, and most importantly, I am always happy and have no attachments. We all care for others and desire to work to contribute to the community the best value and quality products.

Therefore, I offer a simple, easy-to-use roadmap to the community, wishing everyone can apply this mind and achieve happiness and success in life.

PART III: PRACTICE

I. THE BODY PRACTICE, BREATH PRACTICE AND MIND PRACTICE PATH TO ACHIEVE WISDOM

In 1993, after ten years of leaving Long Thien pagoda to go into life, I wrote an explanation to the Venerable Master Hue Thanh. I presented him a practical session about how to train a Vajrayana practitioner with three stages: Body Practice, Breath Practice and Mind Practice to achieve wisdom in this life.

In lectures as well as articles, I have talked a lot about training a person. Training a wise person method is still incomplete. High intellectuals, though successful, cannot maintain and develop that success in the long term and did not exploit all human resources. Though they are able to maintain and continue to grow towards higher success, but there are not many of them who are happy. Because they are bound by that success they lose the freedom of both, body and soul. A wise person is not like that. If there is a wise mind, it will not be bound and will always be awake, aware and intuitive enough to apply the mind of sacrifice, patience, diligent, honest and compassion into work and life so they can achieve the true freedom.

When wisdom has been achieved, it can be applied into intellectuals quickly, but it takes a long time to transform your consciousness from intellectual to wisdom, which is a process without time limitation. After years of practicing and applying the Buddhism philosophy, I saw very clearly the life of Buddha. He enlightened under the Bodhi Tree, at that time he still had not achieved wisdom. He established a path and patiently begged for alms for 49 years to experience what he enlightened. At that time, he achieved complete wisdom. If a person has wisdom, he has to prove it by works. So, my training roadmap for a wisdom person goes through three stages of Body practice, Breath Practice and Mind Practice to enlighten the wisdom sea.

Mindfulness is the first stage of the practitioners. The final destination for practicing mediator is Samadhi stage. However, Buddha left Samadhi and all meditation techniques. He let himself back to natural and normal stage and then the True Mind suddenly appeared. The meditator attains success, then the True Mind and at the same time the wisdom arises. From this wisdom, the practitioner applies with a path of *sacrifice, patience, diligence, honesty and compassion* which is absolutely necessary to develop his own skills and the development of the country. The following is an explanation of the three stages of Body practice, Breath Practice and Mind Practice:

Nama Shakyamuni Buddha

Nama Vairocana Buddha

Nama Bodhisattvas

Dear master

Before I present to you the path of training a Tantric Buddhism practitioner, I want to repent all faults to purify my body, words and mind.

Dear master, The Great Venerable, vice chairman of the Central Dharma Executive Council of Vietnam Buddhist Sangha.

I am Thich Hue Dang, also called Thanh Quang. I repent myself in front of the Venerable master. Please allow me to use this letter as a means to submit my presentation on how to train a Tantric Buddhism practitioner. It is also my experience of 20 years of studying and practicing.

When the master wants to choose a Tantric Buddhism practitioner, he does not distinguish between monks or a layperson that practices Buddhism at home without becoming a monk. If a person wants to be Tantric Buddhism practitioner, he/she has to have the six senses working in good condition and must go through a selection and trial process to vow to devote himself/ herself to Buddha Dharma and the master. He/she will spend at least 3 years after receiving the esoteric transmissions from the master. The master will use these following means to train him/her:

- Firstly, the master will use the Mantrayana Buddhism mantras (Great Compassion Mantra) to open the practitioner's heart. The master will let the practitioner go to a closed room or a Bodhi Mandala (holy site) to preach and teach him directly. After a while, the practitioner must chant the Great Compassion Mantra at least 216 times while sitting in lotus position. He can chant with sound or in silence to get into Samadhi easily. Besides that, the master may teach him the Kunïdïi Bodhisattva sutra. Kunïdïi Bodhisattva sutra is following the mantra yoga method. The practitioner will meditate with the AUM (OM) sound to calm the six causes, six senses and eight consciousnesses. It also takes 12 -18 months for practitioners to repent their sins with Liang Repentance litany. After this practice period, the practitioner has a calm mind and a solid cross-legged (full lotus position) sitting position in at least two hours or more. Thus, the practitioner has been through the body practice with asana yoga or

chanting mantra in lotus position. After the body practice is finished, the practitioners are aware of some wisdom and super power. However, the practitioner often stuck here because he thinks he is good enough. He achieved some wisdom and super power so he often stops here and starts giving lecture or cures diseases then slowly he gave up his practice. There are three more steps for Tantric Buddhism practitioner to go forward. The master will use Prajna Paramita to break the misleading mind and attachment of the practitioner to bring the Tantric Buddhism practitioners to the next period: open the energy center of the body.

There are three steps in the opening energy centers: The opening energy center of the body period is very important to help the practitioner to gain fully enlightened wisdom and be able to see the true nature of all forms. Masters must have a clear and precise vision to identify that the practitioner can meet the three following conditions:

Condition 1: Practitioner has to have calm mind and obtain great compassion.

Condition 2: Practitioner must have some special talents.

Condition 3: Practitioner must have wisdom because the master already preached a part of Prajna Paramita sutra to help him see the true nature of all forms, decreased the misleading mind and attachment.

When the master decides to let the practitioner go to the opening energy centers of the body stage, he will use Kriya Yoga, a breathing discipline to control the energy flows and energy centers in practitioner's body.

Kriyâ Yoga used to be widely popular in India by Lahiri Mahâsaya, Pantanjali, Krishna, Arjuna. Ancient masters also passed it to Christ, St. Jean, St. Paul and the other apostles.

Kriya Yoga is the breathing discipline to control the mind and energy flows. We practice meditating on the sacred word 'AUM'. Pantanjali postulated that God is the vibration in the universe of the holy word OM (or AUM) that the yogis hear during meditation. OM is the creative sound, the engine sound of the universe. The yogis will cultivate that the echoing sound of OM came from the holy place deep within their consciousness. While he received a spiritual encouragement like that, he knows that he has been in contact with the universal energy.

In the stage of the practitioner's mind merging with the divine consciousness as above (Savikalpa Samadhi), the yogi's consciousness will merge with consciousness of the universe. It makes the yogi look, stiff and unmoving, like a dead corpse. However, the yogi is fully aware of the slowing of his body.

Why does master teach this method to the practitioner?

This yoga method helps the yogi connect the Divine Consciousness to his consciousness through breathing practice. It is the treasure of human knowledge and brings more energy to resist diseases caused by the weather. Our vitality is normally wasted by the daily activities. It should be used for the high spiritual activities by practicing yoga to calm the pace of breath.

Once the practitioner has finished the opening body energy stage, in the second period of the step II, the practitioner has to go to a closed room. The master has to build a closed room in a good place. In this period, the master will use his super power to open the energy of practitioner's body, lead his energy flow in the practitioner's body even before he can practice himself. Why? Because this method is dangerous. The practitioner needs to be calm and supported by the master. It is called Sushumna, or Kundalini– the road to enlightenment. These are the three different names, but they are identical.

Sushumna yoga control breathing along the spine to open the inexhaustible energy source in the human body. It helps the practitioner maintain the Samadhi state longer because he has more inner power. He is in the breathing practice state (the second state of opening body energy).

Dear venerable master, I have presented the explanation of the first two stages. The step I uses the Tantric Buddhism Mantra for body practice. The step II is opening the body energy with the three disciplines that I have presented in the two stages above. The first one will control the energy around the body. The second one will lead energy to the backbone. And the third one is called chakra. It opens all resources of the practitioner. These energy sources were stored in energy centers. Its discipline is called the merging divine consciousness discipline or the Samsara escape discipline. It is this last discipline that the master will pass to the Tantric Buddhism practitioner. When the practitioner is in the closed room, the master will use his energy from the emptiness of his mind (True Mind) to open the chakras for the practitioner. Then, he sits in meditation state to focus on these energy centers to open these chakras.

Why does the master have to do that?

The supported energy from the master will keep the practitioner safe from being frenetic. The master plays the most important role in opening up the energy center for practitioners.

Dear venerable master, when the practitioner studies with the Tantric Buddhism master, the master passes to him these disciplines. It called Cittama nitara (empowerment, Initiation ceremony). The practitioner will be challenged and requested to endure the most important test through faith, patience, wisdom and meditation. When practitioner finishes his time in the closed room, the master will allow him to join the others. The master will preach Buddha sutras that include the Mahāvairocana Tantra, Prajna sutra, Lankāvatāra sūtra. These three sutras are very important to a Tantric Buddhism practitioner. Mahāvairocana Tantra is the main sutra of Tantric Buddhism. Prajna Sutra will help you see the true nature of all forms. Lankāvatāra sūtra was given to the second Zen Patriarch Huìkě by Bodhidharma in China. Why do Tantric Buddhism and Zen share this sutra? It is because the Lankāvatāra Sūtra can help the practitioner transform his eight consciousnesses to wisdom. Tantric Buddhism also helps people transform consciousnesses to wisdom. It helps the practitioner attain Buddhahood enlightenment instantly. After finishing practicing with the master, the practitioner will go to a quiet place to practice on his own and finish the last discipline. He will open all his chakras to attain the inexhaustible energy sources and wisdom. Therefore, the Tantric Buddhism practitioner will go from Hinayana to Mahayana. The Hinayana disciplines help the practitioner develop an endurance to merge with the power and principle, and practice of Mahayana.

In short, when the master helps the Tantric Buddhism practitioner to transform from Hinayana to Mahayana, he completes his responsibility of the first phase. These disciplines were applied in many countries such as France, USA, Australia, Canada, China, Tibet, Indonesia and India.

Dear venerable master, I have submitted the itinerary for training a Tantric Buddhism practitioner. I am now moving towards the venerable master who has infinite compassion for all to prove and preach me on the way to complete wisdom. And I also need your help to preach the Buddhist-truth widely, thereby enlightening the sentient beings as your words in Dalat.

Before finishing my presentation, I bow to the Eternally dwelling Triple Gems of the Ten sects to wish you have an auspicious time, and peace of body and mind.

Nama bodhisattvas Mahatat

Nama bodhisattvas Mahatat

Nama bodhisattvas Mahatat

Dalat, 01st March, 1993

Sincerely

Your student

Bhiksu Thich Hue Dang

Two months after sending my explanation, I received a letter from the Venerable Master confirming the path I presented. The following is a letter from the Venerable Master:

Long Thien Pagodas, 30th march 1998

From venerable master Thich Hue Thanh to student Thich Hue Dang in Da Lat

I am very delighted to receive your letter from Da Lat to Long Thien Pagoda to greet and present your explanation on practicing Dharani discipline of Mahavairocana Buddha on the way to enlightenment and emancipation.

Venerable master found that the presentation was clear and had complete principles. Your path is also the path of other successful Zen masters have been through.

The spiritual practice has to go though many stages to achieve Samadhi and Wisdom. You have been through the following stages:

1. *Body practice*
2. *Breath practice*
3. *Mind practice*

Meditators must be patient as many stages that seem easy are actually very difficult to attain. They can get support from the Dharani power to achieve the purpose of their practice; the core issue of the monks is transforming the ignorance to enlightenment. Buddhas and Patriarchs also had been though these stages. And now, we also only follow their path and practice similarly to transform senses to wisdom. It means transforming the eight consciousnesses to four wisdoms, from the first one to the fourth one until you can get the Adarśa-jñāna (Mirror-like Wisdom).

I am very happy that you solidly went through these stages. It is based on the great compassion of the Buddha called Avadhi (The uncaused omniscience of mahavairocana) and achieve ambitions of ones who attain enlightenment for self and others.

I have a few words to praise your diligent practice and urge you to join the Summer Courses that will start from early April to order to preach students and carry on your mission to train the talented monks by widely preaching the Buddha truth.

Wish you peace of mind and more diligence to achieve your goals and wishes.

Your Venerable master

Thích Hue Thanh

Vice chairman of Central Dharma Executive Council of Vietnam Buddhist Sangha.

Over 45 years of my practice, I realized that the people of Vietnam, as well as the international community, must develop their own internal resources. People have an unimaginable power. This internal resource, once opened, will be useful to develop wisdom and skills. The training process that I presented requires a great heart of patience for the practitioner, and the mind of the practitioner also needs to be compatible with the teacher to achieve wisdom.

Thus, the process of training a wise person to be useful for the country is not easy. Planting trees only needs ten years, but it is not sure whether to train a person who takes a hundred years to complete. I have been making Ngoc Linh Ginseng for more than ten years now and have been successful. But to train a truly wise person, I have not yet completed, because I have not found a suitable one in spite of there being enough brave and patient people who can follow my schedule. I always look forward to finding people to train them to be a wisdom person and help the country's development.

II. APPLY MEDITATION AND FIVE HARMONY PRACTICE TO LIFE

According to the Avatamsaka Sutra, in order to preach the cultivation of the Bodhisattva and the Bodhisattva path of accomplishing enlightenment in life, the Buddha went through forty-nine days of meditation to become enlightened with Karmic affinities, and twenty-one days in samadhi to find the direction to lead the way into life. This proves that the sutra existed more than twenty-five centuries before the Buddha had applied Buddhism to life, helping sentient beings escape the affliction of the world to attain salvation and enlightenment.

Thus, Buddhism is not a doctrine for us to study, discuss and debate. Buddhism is a diligent experience and the truth of human life. This path has entered life in a natural way, integrated into every thought and every human action through ages. Buddhism has been endured and developed continuously for over two thousand and five hundred years. Buddhism was born to break ignorance and bring enlightenment. It enlightens everyone on the way to cultivate wisdom and escape from attachment to have a peaceful and happy life. Buddhism helps people overcome themselves, reach the True Life of Contentment, the True Peace in oneself and also the Being, the True Nature of the Universe. Our soul does not suffer from the scenes of lust, anxiety and fear, and achieves a new life of innocence and selflessness in the midst of this vivid and colorful life.

Following the example of Buddha, Zen masters apply meditation to their lives, to benefit their lives, and to bring their religious practice to life to make Buddhism more practical. The characteristics of a Zen are liberal and completely unbound into cumbersome rituals or religious rituals. It mainly focuses on the mind of concentration, to apply to life in a subtle way. This is clearly expressed through the painting and calligraphy works of Japanese Zen sect, also known as Zen masters.

Meditation is an expression of awakening. It transcends ordinary writings that were written in many scriptures. It is personal, but requires the help of a teacher. Meditation has serious features, but is also comfortable. Meditation focuses on reality rather than symbolism. It is the inspiration of many arts. Meditation helps us hear and know in a real way. We will not only think but also feel. We will not let us stop at what we already understand and know. We are willing to accept diversity of the world to meditate and enjoy it.

Meditation art is also the art of awareness. Art works are a way of showing off the inner life of Zen master. Zen Art has a long history of over a thousand years from China. It was brought to Japan in the 13th century. Although China is influenced by Confucianism and Taoism, but Zen art still bears the fruit with an independent and serene nature. There were evident changes in the Japanese politics, economy, and the weakening of the religion, but Zen art still existed and is still increasingly flourishing. In addition to calligraphy and painting, Zen is also expressed through the art of poetry, tea ceremony and flower arrangement. The power of Zen art is generally in its ability to eliminate what is not essential.

Meditation is not just a simple application of Buddhist principles. It is aimed at attaining personal enlightenment by introspection and inner training. The teachings of the Zen school suggest that the desires and rational thinking methods are only illusory and overshadow the existing Buddhahood nature of human beings. Each individual must have a duty to awaken his true nature. To do that, it is crucial to be completely voluntary and guided by a teacher who has attained enlightenment. A Zen practitioner must persist a long and strict training, including many years of meditation before reaching enlightenment which can happen suddenly by a temple bell or a timely whip given by the master. Meditators must follow the five harmony practices.

HARMONY PRACTICES

1. Regulate eating

Buddha sutra said, 'A healthy body brings a healthy mind. Regulate eating, stay in a quiet place. Silent mind will bring diligence mind.'

So, the first thing is to regulate your eating and drinking habits. If you don't eat and drink in the right way, your body will not be stable and your practice will not be effective. Food nourishes our body to cultivate the Buddha path. Although the Buddha philosophy said this physical body is illusory, but we need to rely on this body to cultivate the enlightenment path. It is called using the illusory means to cultivate the Truth, from visibility to invisibility. We have the body, and we need to eat right to nurture this body. Ancients said, 'The Dharma wheel has not moved yet, the food moved first.' It is enough to see that food is an essential need of man.

If you eat too much, your stomach is full, your breath is fast, your veins are inadequate and your mind is stuck, so laziness arises, hundreds of sicknesses arise, your mind and body are not peaceful, and therefore, your enlightenment path also stops.

We should not eat too little. If you eat too little, you are too thin and your mind is hovering. Your thoughts are negative. If the body is already weak, the mind is also suspended. Your mind is not stable. Thoughts are wandering. The body is weak, the spirit is low and afflictions will come to you. How can you practice anything if you have no energy? Thus, eating too much or too little, both will not help you reach Samadhi.

It is necessary to know which things are worth eating and which are not worth eating. If you eat dirty things that make your body sicker and make you sleep more, your afflictions increase. You should not eat bad food because they make the consciousness of a person comatose. If the things that make the body and mind free of illness can increase the path of karma and reduce the path of birth and death, then you should eat. If things do not adapt or stimulate the recurrence of an old disease, causing the four greats against each other it can make you sick. The old saying 'the disease from the mouth' is this meaning.

In short, regulating eating and drinking is not too hungry, not too fully. You must know enough. The first practice of meditation practitioners is to regulate eating and drinking.

2. Regulate sleeping

Sleeping too much will make you ignorant; we should not let go deep into it. If we sleep too much, we will not only abandon the dharma practice of the saints but also lose all the diligence which can cause the mind to be subdued thereby reducing the goodness. We must be enlightened with the impermanence of desire. By regulating sleep and resting, the spirit be clear and so will the mind. So, we can get in to the state of mind of saints, gaining the right concentration. The scriptures say, 'Do not sleep at the end and begin of the night. Do not waste the enlightenment of your life for the desire of sleeping. The fame of impermanence will burn away in vain. One can obtain enlightenment without oversleeping.' Meditation practitioners need to regulate sleep properly. If we sleep too much, our mind will be confused. If we sleep too little, our body will be damaged. So, we need to sleep regularly and correctly. Oversleeping and too much rest are the dark of side ignorance which can be enchanting and cover our lucid spirit. It is necessary to not let the sleeping desire control you, as people who do not oversleep have a clear mind. As for the people who sleep too much, their consciousness loses their awareness. The six consciousnesses are covered by ignorance. People who sleep too much not only abandon the practice but also waste time and their mind gradually becomes gloomy and enchanted.

So, practitioners have to awaken and enlighten the impermanence and self-disciplines. It is necessary to quickly regulate sleep to make the mind bright. Your mind is naturally pure, so that it can be centered on the state of holy scene, and the natural Samadhi will appear.

The scriptures said, 'At the beginning of the night and at the end of the night, do not waste time in sleeping.' It means that the beginning of the night and the end of the night are the best times for practicing meditation. It keeps you alert and awake.

Do not let the desire for sleeping control you and waste the time of your life. Remember to be aware of the flame of impermanence to purify consciousness. The scriptures recorded, 'If we cannot achieve salvation in this life, which life can we do it?' This is a clear and honest teaching which you must take.

After regulating eating and sleeping, there were three more things to be regulated, such as body, breath and mind. However, these three types of practices must be coordinated and cannot be separated.

3. Regulate the body

We neither have to regulate the body to be slow nor hasty, the breath without hissing or slipping and the mind without sinking or getting agitated. Those are the most important practices.

The method of practice comes in the following order- First we regulate the body, then we regulate the breath, and finally we regulate the mind (Body practice, Breath practice, Mind practice). At every stage, we should follow the following steps- Enter – Stay - Export. That is, when we get into Samadhi, it is from a rough to a subtle process. When we get out of Samadhi, it is from a subtle to a rough process. It is the practice process of body, breath and mind.

First, before practicing meditation, you must regulate your body. Practitioners who want to enter Samadhi need to regulate the body. When we walk, stand, lay, sit or act quietly or loudly, we all must be cautious and calm. If the action is rough, the breath is panting, because of the gasp; the mind is scattered, and unable to be quiet and gentle. If the practitioner wants to get into Samadhi, he has to prepare his body first. After entering meditation, your body must be well-informed to be determined.

If all the actions are rough, then the breathing is heavy and the mind is scattered. If the mind is scattered, it is difficult to concentrate. When meditating, there is also a disturbance in the mind that makes you unable to be calm and peaceful. Therefore, practitioners need to understand that even when they are out of concentration, they must bear in mind the practice to regulate the body. Meditation is everywhere and all the time, while walking, standing, laying, sitting and speaking, and in calm and gentle.

When you come to the meditation seat, you have to sit still first. When everything is fine, there is no obstacle. If you sit in the half lotus pose, take your left foot to the right leg, pull it close to your body, and leave your left toes with the right leg thigh so that the foot is equal to the left foot.

If you sit in the full lotus position, you must pull your right foot to cross over the left leg. Then, extend the shirt and waistband to be straightened so that when sitting without being misleading.

Next, place the left hand on the right palm, the fingers overlapping, except for the thumb, then reach the turning point of the foot, pulling it close to the body, stabilizing the center. Adjust the body upright, first move the body and limbs seven or eight times, like the massage method, but don't let the limbs move. Keep it straight, so that the spine does not bend and does not wobble; the neck is straightened, so that the nose and navel are symmetrical, not skewed, not leaning, not bending down or not looking up. Your face is calm and right. The body sitting upright is like a Buddha Statue, not letting the head, body or the limbs fluctuate. It is an initial method of regulating the body when you enter meditation. In short, not slow or rushed, it's a form that regulates the body.

The half lotus pose means the left leg crosses on the right leg. And the full lotus must pull the right foot cross on the left leg. The left hand and the right hand are symmetrical like those of Amitabha mudra. When the arms and legs are already stable, we must consider the operation of the chest. Your spirit is cheerful. Body is neither stubborn nor upright. Head is not bent nor raised, not tilting to the left or to the right. The body is like a Buddha statue, this is the form of Samadhi.

4. Regulate the breath

The breath has four forms: the rough breath, the weak breath, the air breath and the energy breath. The first three breaths are non-harmonious and the fourth is the harmonious form.

What is rough breath? When meditating, we breathe in and out of the nose and we can feel the wind and the sound of the air flow.

What is weak breath? The breath that has no sound, condensation and is not stable is weak breath.

What is the air form? When sitting in meditation, the breath does not make sound, it does not stop, but it is slight and gentle.

What is the energy breath? The breath that has no sound, no condensation, no roughness; the breath in and out is calm and peaceful as if it is lost. The face and mind are in peace.

If you have rough breath, your mind is still wandering and is tired. When your breath come to energy breath, you can gently enter Samadhi.

This is an explanation of how practitioners meditate. After regulating the body, apply the method of breath regulation. Every time you see you suffering from unstable breath or feel uncomfortable in your body and mind, you must adjust it to bring it back to harmony.

If you want to regulate your breathing, you must follow three steps mentioned below:

1. Abandon attachments in your mind

2. Comfort your body

3. Observe your breathing pattern. If the mind is calm, the breath will be gentle. If you keep your breathing in harmony, the affliction thoughts will not arise and you will easily enter Samadhi. Meditators must regulate their breath before entering Samadhi.

If you want to remove the three types of unharmonious breaths such as: Rough, Weak and Air to get into the energy breath, you must follow the three steps mentioned below:

Firstly, remove obstacles and attachments from your mind. Practitioners focus on observing the breath going in and out.

Then your mind observes the breath flow from the nose to the area under the navel.

Secondly, comfort your body. The whole body is natural and relaxed.

Thirdly, your mind follows your energy flow through the body, smoothly without any obstacles.

When you fully implement these three methods from rough to subtle, the mind will be in peace.

5. Regulate the mind

There are three steps to regulate the peace of mind: Enter – Stay – Export.

a) Enter

The enter step has two meanings. The first involves restoring the chaos and not letting your mind wander. The second is regulating the low, high, unstable and hurried breath. If you want to get into Samadhi stage, you have to regulate the mind.

The first step is concentrating your mind in one place and not letting it wander or follow the outside scenes. You must draw back your mind within to observe your breathing.

The second step is regulating your breath from the low, high, slow and hurried state.

The third step is removing the other distractions from outside and your own thoughts. Do not lose your mind in the past and future thoughts. Do not let your mind follow the desire for appearance, sound, smell, taste, touch and ideas. Those things are not a characteristic of a harmony mind. In short, it is possible to make the mind not too low or not too high. It is called the harmony of the mind.

What is a low state? When you are meditating and do not remember anything is when we are in a low state. You like to bow down. At that time, you must pay attention to the tip of the nose and concentrate on your breath. Your mind will not disperse. This can treat the low state.

What is high state? If you are sitting in meditation and your mind is agitated is when you are said to be in a high state. The body is not stable. You remember and think of other things outside. At that moment, you should calmly keep your mind on your belly under the navel, and your mind will calm down.

In a state of concentration, you also have two levels. In the beginning, you are able to subdue the delusional thoughts. You will not dip into a low or high state. It is called heading Samadhi. If you are not careful when you sit, you will immediately fall in the slow and hurried state. These states often happen in concentration step.

The hurried state: This is when the practitioner is sitting still, being mindful and is focused on one concept. This concept is an illusion and not true mindfulness. If this concept is used to be focused, you will feel a throbbing in the chest and your body and mind will not be comfortable. Every time the practitioner is diligent in the concentration state in the body, but the mind is not yet determined and there is a long-suffering chest pain in the body. If you want to treat this disease, you have to let go of that mind and imagine that the energy is going down to the navel. Then, the disease will naturally disappear because this anxiety is due to the overuse of concentration. You can let go of your mind. You bring all the thoughts, confusion, the rough mind and fast breathing to pour down to the navel, not to be directed upwards, it is:

'Stop the fire in your heart,

Release the heat to be cool,

Leave behind a hundred thoughts,

Return to the pure mind' If that is the case, then the mind illness will naturally go away.

The slow state: This is a disease during concentration. That is, at first, the practitioner knows the direction and meaning in the mind, but then, the mind is scattered and cannot concentrate, and the body starts to move and twist. These are signs of suffering and lead unhappiness, sadness, afflictions and confusion in the six senses.

If these diseases are developed during concentration, it is necessary to recognize them early and immediately expose them to the body and to observe that mind, not to let the mind go outside, making the mind remain at one point. The slow state is because of lack of diligence. If the mind still recites and pays attention to a scene called drawing the six consciousnesses and continuously destroy the thoughts. The spirit is elated and does not let the mind be lazy. If you take these things that are good medicine to treat the disease, the slow state disease will be eliminated from the root.

While concentrating and going deeper in meditation, you face more subtle diseases. Usually, meditation is from the rough to subtle. The body is crude, the breath is in it, and the mind is very subtle. Regulating from crude to subtle will calm your mind. This is the original means of concentrating and is also known as the reconciliation of two things when you first enter meditation.

The method of Samadhi is the rough to the subtle. In the beginning, you regulate the body, then you regulate the breath, finally you regulate the mind. Because the body is rough, it is needed to be practiced first and then feel the breath in it. The mind is very subtle, so it is the final step of the practice. It is meaning from rough to subtle then the thought will not arise which is called skillfully regulating the mind and destroying the afflictions. This is the first method to enter Samadhi.

b) Stay

During the state of meditation, we have to regulate the things - body, breath and mind. Practitioners can meditate for 2 hours, or 4 hours or 6 hours in the 24 hours of the mindfulness state. During that time, you have to be aware of the harmony of three things– the body, the breath and the mind. When you are sitting, if the body is either hot or inclined, or bent down or looking up, or the body is not upright, you should know it and immediately correct it so that the body can be peaceful. Adjust the body and do not be lazy or overcontrolling. It should be natural; stay peaceful and stable.

When a practitioner meditates, from the moment of entering into Samadhi to the time off, however long or short, contemplation and mindfulness are used. Contemplation is drawing all thoughts into one point to purify your mind from illusions.

When the mindfulness is used, it is necessary to know the three things– the body, the breath, and whether the mind is harmony. It must be clear. You have to harmonize the body, not let it be lazy and not restrain it. If you can regulate the breath that is not too scary, not too slippery, thoughts are submerged and not emerge. This case is called harmony, otherwise, the body is not said to be in harmony. In the beginning, people could sit up straight and practice meditation. But after sitting for a long time, they get tired physically and mentally, and either other thoughts arise or the body starts to lose status and cannot retrain posture, thereby leaning, bending down or looking up, and sometimes becoming unsteady and moving. These are not signs of a straight body and mind. We need to fix it immediately to keep your mind stable. During that time, there are no lazy or controlled ways.

When practitioners are meditating, they observe their body and breath. They have to check whether they are in the low, high, slow or hurried state or not. If they have these diseases, they will apply the above method to adjust it. They move their mind towards the navel, preventing all illusions and thoughts.

In short, while meditating, you have to remember to keep your body, breath and mind in harmony. Three things combine into one body. When body and the breath are not contradicting, the mind does not go wandering and overcomes all obstacles, and then the path of meditation can be natural achieved.

c) Export

When the meditation period is about to finish, you should let go of your mind, open your mouth to let one breath out of your mouth. Then, you should think of the hundreds of blood vessels that are in moving lightly in your body. Then, move your neck and both your legs. Rub your hands all over the pores. Rub your hands against each other until they are hot and put them on your two eyes, then, open your eyes and wait for the heat in your body to fade away before ending the meditation process. If you do not do so, when you sit, you can stay quiet in the mind, but if you come out quickly, the subtle thoughts have not melted and stay in the body, causing headaches, hundred joint pains and other pains. Later, while sitting in meditation, there is no peace. Therefore, if you want to get out of the meditation state, it must be a subtle to rough process. This is the method of regulating the body, the breath and the mind when it comes out. Thus, it is called skillful enter, stay and out as a verse:

Progress is in order

Rough is not contrary to subtle

Like controlling a horse

In and out in order.

This section explains clearly that when one comes out of meditation, it is necessary to regulate the body, the breath and the mind. If you want to get into concentration, it must be from rough to subtle. When you want come out, it must be from subtle to rough.

This is a method of regulating body, breath and mind. The Lotus Sutra said, 'The masses and the bodhisattvas have been in countless thousands of lives, only because of the Buddha's path, you should be diligent and clever in entering, staying and getting out to thousands righteousness concentration, being of great mind, has long happy pure appearance and practice meditation in order.' This is a quote from the Lotus Sutra to testify this method. This sutra is the last of the Buddha and discussing in detail the five times, explanations on the teachings of the meditation method, showing non-dual disciplines. However, those spiritual practices, there are disciplines that do not regulate the body, the breath and the mind, and at the same time, enter, stay and export. Buddhas in the past have followed these disciplines so that, in the future, they can continue the same practice. Buddhas in past, present and future all practice like that.

The gates to the True mind are through the senses, eyes, ears, nose, tongue, body and thoughts (mind). There are many meditating techniques that we can apply to go into this state of mind.

III. VAJRAYANA YOGACARA MEDITATION

You can practice this method everywhere and anytime because your eyes are still open while you are practicing. In the beginning, you should practice the Vajrayana yogic meditation in sitting position.

1. Preparation for location and time

Meditation, yoga and Pranayama which are the purposeful practice methods that use breath to tame the senses and concentrate the mind to master the central nervous system (master the motor nervous system, master the feeling, sensory, cerebral cortex, hippocampus, hypothalamus, autonomic nervous system), thereby mastering the two states of the nervous system "excitement and inhibition", practicing to create new conditioned reflexes and eliminating bad conditional reflections which were created by the environment.

A better preparation will help us practice better. Beginners need a relatively quiet environment. If we sit in a loud noisy place, it will make the auditory nerves tired. Soft noises make it easy for us to fall sleep, whereas loud noises stimulate the nerves. We get distracted and can't control our breathing which leads to a change in our heart beat. Practitioners must not be entangled in both body and mind.

You have to be completely relaxed, forget everything, and completely focus on your practice. The unstable mental, joy, sadness, mourning and hatred also affects the nerves and endocrine glands, the organs (according to stimulation, the brain can release endorphins, a type of Endogenous morphine to limit the activity of nerve cells related to pain, feeling relaxed and soothing. The brain releases pheniletilamine that acts like an amphetamine drug (the famous stimulus is Maxiton). When the brain releases pheniletilamine, we will feel less hungry, less sleepy, less tired and more playful and active. With a good preparation, we can sit for a long time (sitting in a comfortable and pleasant manner where the practicing sessions will give us good results).

1.1 Prepare location for Meditation

We should have a separate room to meditate and must not let the outsiders get into that space in order to maintain a solemn atmosphere. The room must be well ventilated (with windows). Ventilation means that the air can flow; the oxygen in the air in the room must be 21%. If we sit in a place that lacks oxygen, we will quickly get tired because breathing is difficult. We cannot reach the feeling of ease and comfort. Our nervous system will be disordered because we have to pay much attention to control the breath and the heartbeat. The blood pressure and organs are also affected. There is a cushion pad to sit on it (sitting tool).

The sitting place must ensure no wind or rain. If you sit in the place where the wind can get through, your body will become cold. When that happens, the body tries to maintain normal body temperature by enhancing oxidation and reducing heat by contracting the peripheral blood vessels to transport blood into the internal organs. Therefore, this sudden change affects heart rate and blood pressure. If our nerves do not adjust or adapt to the changes in time, we can easily get cold which can cause cold sweats, fainting and even convulsions.

The sitting place must not be too bright or too dark. If we sit in a bright spot, it makes us dazzled to stimulate nerves. We are distracted and unable to control the breath in a gentle and comfortable manner, which also makes us tired.

The sitting place must be not cold or too hot. If we sit in a hot place, it requires more effort for the body. The blood circulation increases and so does the oxygen consumption, thereby increasing the rate of respiration. The body has to work more to keep the heat balance. Upon overheating, the body will have a burning sensation in the skin, shortness of breath, thirst, headache and excessive sweating which will cause the electrolyte in the brain to vibrate. The brain will get worse. The body will be less active and tired because the brain's impulses affects the metabolism in the body cells and reduces concentration. The loss of water by sweating increases the protein level of the blood, making the blood thin and increasing the blood pressure, causing blood circulation disorders in the brain. This will lead to adverse effects on the brain in the long term.

Do not sit near a fireplace because the fire will make your body hot and the smoke will suffocate you. If there is too much CO_2 in the air, it will affect respiration and cause heart diseases and heart attacks in the long term.

Do not sit near water beside the sea. The air entering the alveoli is saturated with water vapor, at least 98% at body temperature, under a pressure of 47 mm Hg. It is calculated that the body must provide 700 ml of water daily to air into the alveoli. At high temperatures, the saturation of air vapor will decrease, so if we sit in hot and humid places it will cause the body an unpleasant 'stress', especially when the heart is weak.

Do not sit when it is thunderous. Practicing meditation under the thunderstorms will adversely affect the body because when the air pressure changes, the lack of oxygen component in the air will cause difficulty in breathing, chest tightness, and bad effects to the cardiovascular and mental systems. The thunder also irritates the nervous system, makes us tired quickly and affects the heart rate and blood circulation. It will cause bad effects on the body in the long run.

1.2 Best practice time

All yogis from the deep caves and forests to the high and snow-covered mountain enter the Samadhi form between 2:00 am and 5:30 am. That is the basic meditation time. There are also other meditation sessions that depend on the individual decision of the person. So, if possible, we should choose the time between 2:00 am and 5:30 am to enter Samadhi, hope to connect our energy with that of all other yogis on this globe and also hope that these blessings will support us on the path of meditation. In the Lankavatara philosophy, Buddha said, "*At the beginning of the night, at midnight, and in the morning, you will be able to enter into holy wisdom places.*" Therefore, the best time to practice is at midnight (11am-1pm), early in the evening (5pm-7pm), and dawn (4am-6am).

2. Preparation for the body

Before practicing meditation, we have to clean the body (you should go to toilet before the practicing time) and drink a glass of warm or cool water, depending on the season. If you are full, you should not practice. It takes at least two hours after eating to practice because when you are full, the blood pressure increases.

If we practice meditation, it will lower the blood pressure which will lead to a full stomach and indigestion.

A balanced diet of proteins, carbohydrates, fats, vitamins and minerals is very necessary for meditation practice. Barley, fresh fruit, cereals, green vegetables and a few dairy products if needed, that's the suggestion. It is most effective if we can be vegetarian.

Follow the rules of not smoking, drinking alcohol, or using drugs.

We must wear loose clothing as tight clothes will cause discomfort distraction and will be hard to reach a quiet state.

We must practice continuously and on time. Each practice must be carefully prepared; it needs to follow a certain sequence to gradually build and reinforce conditional reflexes of practice. Thus, we will practice better and it will be easier to achieve better results. When it has become a habit (or good conditional reflexes), we should not arbitrarily change.

a . Sitting position

Depending on one's body condition, the practitioner can immediately sit in Padmâsana (cross-legged – lotus position). If you cannot do it, you can practice with a half lotus position or use physical yoga exercises (asana) to support you until you can sit in the lotus position. The goal is sit for at least 2 hours per practicing session.

We should not face the West or South. The North and the East have a good influence on the linear universe.

The backbone must always be straight. If your back does not usually stand upright, then it does not work. Later, if we enter the breathing practice, we cannot transfer energy along the spine; the circulation of the energy flow becomes very slow and very difficult.

a) Padmāsana- the lotus position (cross-legged)

It is called Padmâsana, the lotus position or the cross-legged position. Padmasana has numerous health benefits for mental, physical and spiritual energy. It helps increase circulation in the lower spine, energize and tone abdominal muscles and organs and increases flexibility and strength in the hips, ankles and legs.

How to practice:

- Sitting on the cushion pad with your legs extended out, keeping your spine straight with your arms resting by your side.Now, bend your left knee so that you can cross your left ankle over the top of your right shin. The bottom of your left foot should also face towards the sky. The top of your foot and ankle should rest where your hip bends.
- Bring your knees together as close as possible. Push your midsection toward the floor and sit up straight. Press the outer edges of your feet down onto your thighs, lifting the outer ankles. This will ease pressure between your shins.
- Inter lock your hands in front of your belly and lay down comfortably or bring your hands into Gyan Mudra (Wisdom

Seal) by joining the index finger and thumb on each hand. Extend the other fingers, but keep them together. This will calm you while you pause for a few meditating breaths.

- Open your eyes and look in one point firmly.
- Once you are ready to finish, release the full lotus pose very carefully and slowly by gently extending both legs along the floor. As you maneuver out of the lotus position, pause at each step for a few minutes to meditate.

The lotus position is very balanced, firm and long-lasting, but at the beginning of the test, it is harder to sit than in the meditation (Siddhâsana) written below.

b) Siddhasana - the half lotus in sitting meditation (semi-cross-legged).

This position regulates the two positive and negative currents, so the nervous system is thus gentle, bright and lucid. The brain will develop sequentially depending on the time and ability of the practitioner.

This is an easier way to meditate. It is for practitioners who cannot practice the lotus position.

Padmâsana – Lotus position

The physical and mental usefulness is less than the lotus position. But it is also very useful.

How to practice:

- Sitting on the cushion pad with your legs extended out, keep your spine straight with your arms resting at your side.
- Bend your left knee and hug your knee to your chest. Now, bend your left knee so that you can cross your left ankle over the top of your right shin.
- Cross your right ankle beneath your left knee.
- Inter lock your hands in front of your belly and lay down comfortably or bring your hands into Gyan Mudra (Wisdom Seal) by joining the index finger and thumb on each hand. Extend the other fingers, but keep them together. This will calm you while you pause for a few meditating breaths.
- Open your eyes and look in one point firmly.

Hold up for the duration of your meditation or Pranayama practice.

Release the pose by extending both legs parallel to the floor.

c) Yoga Mudra

The basic yoga mudra position supports you to sit in Padmasana position better. This is the basic posture of Buddha Yoga which is applied before and after each meditation practice. The goal is to keep the energy flow along the spine to the brain. It also helps to open the hips and bring the legs in the lotus position. It is good for long meditation and blood circulation before discharging the meditation session.

How to practice:

- Sitting in the lotus or half lotus position.
- Put both your hands bind behind your back, left hand holding right wrist, inhale to lift up your chest then exhale to release the air and back to relaxing position.
- Inhale slowly and lower your head forward until the forehead touches the ground, hold your breath for as long as possible (hold breath).

- Exhale slowly and take off as you begin to breathe in.
- Practice it in the counts of 7 – 21- 49 –10 per session, up to your time and condition.

Usefulness: This position is a remedy for constipation and stimulates the nervous system. Treatment of rheumatism the circulation is fresh.

3. The detoxification of breath before meditation

Before meditating we should do breathing exercises and some yoga positions. The nose should be cleaned before the session. You must always breathe through your nose and never breathe through your mouth unless for some special exercises instructed by your master.

After controlling the posture and relaxing the whole body, we begin to take a deep, long breath to fill the abdomen (we count the number during the inhalation: for example, from 1 to 10).

Then, we open our mouth to exhale slowly and softly until we run out of breath, and we empty the stomach (we count the number of times we exhale: for example, from 1 to 20). When you inhale and exhale, do not let yourself suffocate so that you do not have to inhale or exhale too quickly, which is how you must feel comfortable and ease.

We continue to breathe seven to eight times. This method of breathing is for discharging bad air.

The purpose of this breathing is to expel all the CO_2 left in the lungs and bring oxygen into the body fully to neutralize the lactic acid remaining in the blood and cells in the body so that we are no longer tired. We will then feel relaxed and comfortable and will be able to sit and practice for a long time and not be distracted.

4. How to practice

The Institute of Vietnam Buddha Yoga Research and Application is practicing Vajrayana Yogacara Meditation. It is the ultimate meditation practice of Tantra to help us realize our supreme ego. This is the ultimate meditation method for yogic meditation from Diamond Sutra by Buddha, so there is a need for a certified master to guide.

When practicing the Vajrayana Yogacara Meditation, the practitioner must go through a physical process to eliminate toxins and be able to sit firmly in a cross-legged position. The

Yoga Mudra Position

lotus position requires to straighten your back. We have to sit cross-legged so that the body does not budge; the energy is balanced and the mind is quiet. We open our eyes to see the lotus flower in front of us from 1.5 m (or choose any fixed point). Your eyes are opening meanwhile your mind is drawing back inside your body. Our eyes open to look at the lotus but do not raise any thought to initiate color or discrimination. We are still awake and aware of everything. We will train the eyes to open the third eye chakra to have the tuition. This is the practice of tantric enlightenment.

You should not have any discrimination to the outside or any attachments in your mind when your eyes catch onto any images.

While our eyes are open and are looking at the lotus, our two ears are listening to the lecture or any sound, but we are not predestined. Our knowing goes back inside. The eyes do not blink, the ears do not follow the sound, but we know it all. When the eyes are set and the ears are fixed, the mind is tranquil. We see and hear everything without the mind chasing after sight and sound.

The lotus is a scene, we face it directly. Sound is the scene is the bar. Large eyes are focused on the lotus. They are the means for us to practice. When any thought arises in your mind when you face the outside factor, you apply the mind of sacrifice, patience and diligence to leave the discrimination and attachment to it. You practice it when you sit in the lotus pose or anytime, or anywhere, then slowly there is a silence and peace in the mind. Then, you are in the stage of the Buddha mind. It means you are transforming the eyes consciousness to Buddha wisdom.

Vajrayana Yogacara Meditation is about controlling the six senses. If you can quiet the thoughts that arise because of the six consciousnesses, it means you are able to pacify the mind. Then, there are six doors (six consciousnesses) to get into the true mind and gain wisdom. You are opening your eyes to face the outside world, but inside you are secretly meditating. You will keep yourself awake and aware, and you will have intuition and enlightened wisdom of the True Mind.

If you keep meditating with your eyes open, your knowing is drawn back inside to practice your breath, you will gain inner power.

Breathing practice and how to manage the energy flow

Level 1:

We breathe naturally, rhythmically, steadily in a relaxed manner stretching out our body. We keep the feeling of comfort and lightness of the whole body. We create emotions of joy, peace and keep this feeling throughout the meditating sessions. We breathe naturally and steadily 5 to 10 times.

When we breathe, our knowing (mind) follows the flow of inhalation of the breath from the nose to the abdomen, and the exhalation of the breath from the abdomen to the nose.

Level 2: Inhale -pause - exhale in the rhythm 2 - 4- 2

Next, check your breath for the right rhythm. These are the two points of the body and the mind regulation that meditator must always watch while meditating in order to control the mind, before proceeding to the stage of mindfulness.

Each meditation session is at least half-an-hour (30 minutes) long. In the beginning, if the body is numb or painful, then you can divide it into two sessions (15 minutes each). We should not put in excessive effort or force the body because meditation is a long-term practice. If you force your body, it will be unsustainable.

In the middle of the practice, if the mind is disturbed with wandering thoughts then you gather it back in your body. You use your mind to scan and check the state of the body, review the head, neck and spine to be upright and come back to your breath.

When you feel sleepy, you widen your eyes, stretch your back a few times, move a few times on your hips, and adjust your back upright and get back to your breath.

If you feel that your heartbeat is rising up too fast, you should give up everything and discharge the meditation. It is a sign that you are sitting in the wrong posture or breathing in a wrong rhythm which is causing bad symptoms to occur in the body. We should give up all the previously practiced (wrong) methods and restart from the basics.

At the beginning of practicing, if the body is numb, focusing on controlling the breath can make your mind tired. If you feel a state of heavy tension on your head, then you should rest and not force yourself too much. If you force your body or mind you will be distracted. Your nerves will be excited and the practice will not bring good results. You should not try too hard in the beginning.

You will encounter many obstacles and difficulties such as numbness, tiredness and discomfort when trying to control the energy. If you are patiently practicing for a long time, you will overcome all obstacles. If you maintain the practice, do not interrupt, maintain punctuality and follow the right method, then you will surely achieve the results as per your wish.

With enthusiasm to remember, identify, learn, distinguish for the right, resolutely giving up all to pursue one purpose sooner or later, you will soon reap results.

The ineffective concentration is due to inadequate breathing, lack of rhythm, numbness in the body, aches and pains, mental distress and irritation.

We sit still for a long time to free the mind from desire. In your mind, you keep observing the five consciousnesses (eyes, ears, nose, tongue and body).If you keep practicing a long time you will create the inner resources for yourself.

This is the ultimate meditation by Naropa (Indian Buddhist Mahasiddha). Sakya Muni Buddha was the one who practiced this meditation method. When he meditated, his eyes opened and the energy was converging to chakras and formed the force of meditation.

When you practice this technique, you will encounter favorable circumstances and hardships, but you will overcome them all. Because, though the eyes are wide open looking at all, knowing everything, and the ears are hearing all the sounds, they cannot disturb you. Your knowing comes back inside, settling in your quiet mind. Since then, a new intuition has been revealed.

Vajrayana Yogacara Meditation is a method to bring the practitioner from awakening (awakening to the six senses/ six consciousnesses of eyes, ears, nose, tongue, body and mind) to awareness (sense of knowing), and then to intuition and enlightenment that is the pure mind and the Buddha mind. So, this is the method of meditation to open the Buddha mind and achieve the wisdom of your own True mind. In order to cultivate this method, you have to practice under the instruction of an enlightened master.

IV. KRIYA YOGA

Kriyâ Yoga discipline used to be widely popular in India and was practiced by Lahiri Mahâsaya, one of the most famous Indian gurus. The word Kriyâ in Sanskrit, meaning making and action; *kri* means karma dhatu, the natural principle of cause and effect. Kriyâ Yoga means to 'Merge with Divine Consciousness thought a ritual or action'. It is the small universal merging with the whole universal.

Yoga believes that a human being is a small universal and we can unite with the contemporary universe and get the energy from it. Through experience, rituals and practices of the author, we can see that this yoga discipline is very important. There is no one in Vietnam but the author who masters this discipline. If no one inherits it, this discipline will be ruined.

A yogi who practices this discipline correctly will slowly be freed from the bondage of karma. Karma was created from your actions of the past life and the present life. Why? Practicing Kriyâ Yoga will solve problems or transform the 8th sense. The 8th consciousness is called Alaya-vijnana. If we can transform it to the emptiness, it is same with Samadhi. If a yogi practices this discipline for a span of two years, he can get into a Samadhi state within two minutes. It is a short cut to the Samadhi. The condition is that you have to prepare for your body first. The only one who can teach Kriyâ Yoga is a competent guru. If you practice it yourself you are risking your own life.

Kriyâ Yoga is a simple discipline of both spiritual and physical being. The spiritual is the True Mind, and the physical is your health. It is requested that the practitioner's health and True Mind receive this discipline. Yoga helps you detox yourself and flush out the toxins and absorb the fresh air into your blood. The toxins will be excreted through 84,000 pores. The toxins that are excreted from the body will have a foul smell. This smell will be gone after seven days. Currently, we can use technology to eliminate toxins from our body which saves a lot of practicing time. This additional element will transform into a Prana to restore vitality in the brain and the spinal cord. This yoga discipline will obtain the pure air from the universe and turn into *ojas* and *ete* to nurture the brain cells and open intellectuality. The highly evolved Yogis can change their cells into the pure crystal matters.

The Yogi can delay or prevent the aging of cells by preventing the accumulation of black blood. When we are getting old, we have more black blood and lack of fresh blood in our bodies. It makes the blood flow slower and slows down the whole system. If you practice this yoga discipline, you can use pure crystal air from the sky. When you practice, your breath will be longer and your body will brighten up.

Buddhism is not praying to any god. The Buddhism truth was discovered and passed by Siddhārtha Gautama. However, the practice of it is Hinduism. We must practice our body and breathe using the yoga discipline first to have better health. Buddhist practitioners should understand that breathing practice is to control your breath and make it longer.

When we practice asanas, breathing and meditation, we will gain mind power. This power can be used in order to help people from a distance, it might be called stealth. The author can stay in Da Lat and work in America, Ha Noi or Saigon at the same time. Buddhism called stealth is Nirmana (the manifest transformation body). Yoga calls it mind power because it is created from mental resources. When you are in Samadhi the power will be there.

Kriyâ Yoga is an ancient yoga that Lahiri Mahasaya learned from guru Babâji who discovered and adjusted this yoga discipline after centuries of being lost in oblivion. Babâji said to Lahiri Mahâsaya, "The Kriyâ Yoga discipline that I propagate to people in the 19th century through you was taught by Krishna. Pantanjali guru, Christ, St. Jean, St. Paul and the other apostles also knew this discipline.' After 40 years of practicing this discipline, the authors adjusted the practice, shortened the time and initiated the combustion stage.

Krishna, a great Indian prophet, mentioned the Kriyâ Yoga in the Bhagavad Gita Sutra. 'The others transfer the Prana through inhalation and exhalation, in the breathing practice called Pranâyama.' This saying means, 'Yogis prevent aging of the body by invigorating vitality and prevent growth through excretion. By neutralizing the aging and growth of the body, and regulating the pace of the heartbeat, the yogi masters the secrets of life and death issuse.'

When the pure air is added into the Ying and Yang air flow, the pure air will go out through the backbone. Breathing from backbone can open up three chakras that can convert fresh air to *ete* through the backbone to feed the brain cells. The goal of this practice is to rejuvenate the brain cells. So, the yogi can master the secrets of life and death issues.

Krishna also said that in a past life, he had taught this yoga discipline for Vivasvat, an enlightened one in the ancient times who taught Lord Manu, the founder of the Indian law. He passed it to Ixvaku, the founder of the India monarch dynasty. Kriyâ Yoga was passed from century to century through the word of mouth and was preserved over time to the era of materialism. Because the ancient monks embrace it in a veil of secrecy and also because most of people do not care about the ancient disciplines, this sacred discipline has gradually disappeared.

This discipline is not for everyone. Will he serve the community after completing this discipline? Who can inherit this discipline? He must prove that he has the True Mind (Buddha mind). This discipline must be taught to people who serve the community. If you want to use it you have to have your inner power. You must find a guru to help you and have the honesty.

People must have the virtue and wisdom; virtue to enlighten people, and the wisdom to help people. It is the virtue and wisdom power, and not the power from any means. If people are always looking for other powers, they cannot understand and succeed. We should not be superstitious; burning incense is the merit thanksgiving to Buddhas who preach the Buddhism truth. We do not pray for help from him.

When you practice any discipline, you can take a short cut for the theory of it but you cannot get the practical results immediately. You have to sacrifice, have patience and diligence to practice this discipline.

Pantanjali guru wrote, 'Kriya Yoga disciplines include: discipline of the body, thought control, and meditation of the sacred word AUM.' Pantanjali postulated God, that is the vibration in the universe of the holy word OM (or AUM) that the yogis hear during meditation. Om is the creative noun, the engine sounds of the universe. The yogis who will have time to cultivate the echoing sound of OM came from the holy place deep within their consciousness. While he received a spiritual encouragement like that, he knows that he has been in contact with the spiritual realm. Before practicing this discipline you have to chant OM.

In this stage of the practitioner's mind merging with the Divine consciousness as above (savikalpa Samadhi), the Yogi's consciousness is merging in the consciousness of the universe.

There is no easier path in this discipline. Because of we take the energy from the outside. The normal breath cannot bring you this energy, but a yoga master can guide you to open these energy centers. You will get into Samadhi faster with Kriya Yoga more than normal meditation if you have a guru to help you open these energy centers.

The vigor externally escapes the body. It makes the yogi look like a dead body, stiff and unmoving. The Yogi is fully aware of the slowing of his body. He has achieved the other higher state (Nirvikalpa samadhi). His consciousness is in harmony with the Divine Consciousness while still awake and fully aware of everything going on around. It is different with the Hinayana meditation; they press their awareness down and make them look like wood or rock when they are in Samadhi.

In everyday activities, effects of Yoga appear suddenly. Sometimes, the chakras below the navel rotate to give signals of future events. It makes your body stiff, but you are still aware of everything and work as usual. The True Mind appears and you feel the pure peace of mind. If you can get into True Mind, you will know everything. You will not blink an eye but your body will still work normally. Now, your Chakra returns to natural state and you have the power from the True Mind. When the author got cancer in 2012, doctors required surgery but the author refused. He used the fire of Samadhi to burn the cancer cells. After two weeks, when he came back for health check again, the cancer was gone. Then, when he met someone with cancer, he could use his Samadhi fire to help them.

Sri Yukteswar said to his students,

'Kriyâ Yoga is a discipline to urge the human evolution. From ancient times, the gurus discovered this secret; the universal consciousness is closely connected with the control of breath.'

When you practice yoga, you are connecting with the universe. Control breathing, you can drag the power of the universe into your body. When the author practiced this discipline in his sleep, he could feel the air flow move through the energy centers and was able to guess the time correctly. This is not superstition. It is the mind power of human being united with the universe. This discovery is the immortal and unique contribution of India into the wealth of knowledge of mankind. The source of human energy and the human vitality is normally wasted by the daily uproar. During the day, we work and talk a lot, and that makes the mind power dissipation. When the night falls, the energy centers work and recreate the power of the mind. The energy centers can recreate energy themselves. It produces the excitation source - the energy for body. Human bodies have a fire energy element including earth, water, air and fire to generate for themselves. If the body has enough energy, it works very well.

If the yogi practices continuously, within one day and night, he will earn the spiritual evolution equivalent a thousand years of natural evolution, and if he practices in one year the result will be equivalent to that of 365,000 years.

The beginners who follow Kriyâ Yoga disciplines should only practice from 14 to 28 circles each time, twice per day. A yogi normally completes his practice in 6 years, 12 years, 24 or 48 years. The yogi who dies before reaching the supreme goal will bring a good karma from meticulous cultivation in the past. In the next life, he will have better conditions to continue practicing until successful.

The body of a human being is compared to a 50-watt bulb. It cannot bear a one million voltage caused by over practicing the Kriyâ Yoga. The increase sequential and reasonable increase in the practice of the Kriyâ Yoga will slowly change the body as you can stand the powerful force of the universe, the first manifestation of the spirit.

In short, Kriyâ Yoga is a discipline to urge human evolution. From ancient times, the gurus have discovered this secret and that the universal consciousness is closely connected with the control of breath. It is the immortal and unique contribution of India into the wealth of knowledge of mankind. The source of human energy and human vitality is normally wasted by the daily uproar. It must be summed up for the high spiritual activity through practicing yoga to calm pace breath.

How to practice:

Sit comfortably in lotus or half lotus pose.

Place the tip of index finger of the right hand in between the eyebrows, the thumb on the right nostril, middle on the left nostril, and the thumb on the right nostril.

Example: Start with a very long exhalation from both the lungs to throw out the carbon dioxide. Press your thumb down on the right nostril (Do not press the nostril with the middle finger) and slowly inhale 4 seconds from the left nostril (the thumb is still pressing the right nostril), press the middle finger on the left nostril and hold your breath in 16 seconds.

Lift the thumb on the right nostril up and breathe out 8 starts (middle finger is pressing the left nostril) to breathe inside the 8 seconds (middle finger while pressing the left nostril), keep it still and inhale from the right nostril 4 seconds.

Now, press both nostrils and hold your breath in 16 seconds. Open the left nostril and exhale in 8 seconds (the right nostril is still closed).

Here is the coordinated breath. Keep this status and continue to do it again. Slowly from the left nostril with 4 seconds and so on. In the beginning, each time is 5 cycles. In a few days, without any reaction in the body, you will be able to increase it to 7 cycles. Every time you add up only one cycle, do not underestimate this reminder.

Take your hand off (do not press your nose anymore) but still breath in and out in the left and the right nostril as your will. Now it is time to let your mind leading your breath into the spine.

IV. SUSHUMNA YOGA OR BREATHING IN THE SPINE DISCIPLINE

The enlightened yogis can breathe in their spine. The patriarch of Raja Yoga concluded, 'Who can breathe in the spine will be enlightened.'

Breathing in the spine is about running your breath along the spine. It is as follows: The backbone has 33 vertebras overlapping each other to create the spine. The spinal cord has a special shape, if slice it up and looks like the number 8 with 2 empty pipes- The left one is called Ida-Nadi, the yin pipe, and the right one is the Pingala-Nadi, the Yang pipe. In the middle, is the marrow which the Yogis call Sushumna path (omniscient, all-knowing path). When the yogis can open this pipe to let the Kundalini (the fire snake) rise upward and unite it with a thousand petals of the lotus energy center called Sahasrara on the top of the head, it mean he has reached his destination.

Sushumna Yoga controls the breath in three empty pipes: Ida Nadi, Pingala Nadi và Sushumna Nadi. Yogis will follow an esoteric breath discipline to control the breath in these three pipes following a mysterious method to reach the supreme paranormal powers.

The yogis have to adhere to vegetarianism, celibacy and must be taught by a competent guru. Otherwise, the yogis can be in danger. They may become frantic or even die as a result of intense reactions.

Following this yoga discipline, the yogis will open the one thousand petals of the lotus energy center with Kundalini, also known as the fire snake. Kundalini is symbolized as a snake so that it you will see how venomous it is. If the yogis do not know the method to tame it or control it without opening it too soon, the yogis will suffer from the harmful consequences before receiving help from the practitioners. If you want to go deeper into this discipline, you have to research and collect information until you fully master the first step, then you can move on. There is an old yoga saying, 'search it, meet it or look for it, and get it' or 'you will if you want'.

With Sushumna Yoga discipline, you just know the three main Nadis: Ida, Pingala and Sushumna. They all stem from one central point called the Kanda, which is located in the middle of the anus. All follow along inside the marrow.

Ida and Pingala are two nerve impulses They are not symmetrical (symetrie) as the nerves in physiology, but are naturally opposites.

Ida is on the left, ending at the left nostril, symbolizing the moon, it is Yang, the operation of Prana, which is the way that leads to Prajna (Prajna: Wisdom).

Pingala is on the right, ending at the right nostril, symbolizing the Sun, the operation of the Apana, which led to Upaya (skillful means). Apana is the manifestation of Prana.

Ida and Pingala is the stream of operation in everyone. We complete all the functions of life because of them. When they join into each other, it is Pranayama (Control breathing).

Sushumna is running in the spinal cord to the ventricle of the brain. It is made of three layers. From the outside to the inside, the three layers represent the moon, sun and fire: Dhustara, vajrini or vajra (lightning of Siva) and cinitri like spider silk, illuminated when the OM sound comes. Only the gurus have this ability.

Asimou wrote in his book, the Jsaac Le cerveau (Marabout, 1965), "In human body, the spinal cord does not fully occupy the length of the cylinder. It stops at the first vertebra or the second, and the canal ependimaire; sometimes the narrow tube disappears in mature men".

Vivekananda said that this empty tube is the Sushumna, and the Sushumna continues where the spine ends, the subtle fibers are shown out of the spinal cord, but here, it is much smaller and is sealed off in the lower end, which is located near the spare modern physiology that can tell triangular shape. The Sushumna is clogged in a normal man so that its impact is not obvious. Only the guru can clear the Sushumna tube and reach the super consciousness. The primary goal of the yogis is to clear the Sushumna.

He gave an example - If a human being wants to transfer the electric, he will need to go through one line. The Mother Nature does not need a physical line, such as lightning (The nature of Sushumna is vajra). These lines in the body are like 'the feeling fibers' and they move in the Ida and Pingala of the guru. They arc the main artery in the centripetal and centrifugal. Why does the spirituality go without a wire? Yogis say that if we can do that, we are no longer in slavery of the physical world. How? The story will be completed here if you make the stream that runs through the Sushumna. The mental systems create nerve nets so that we will no longer need to work through any wires. Then all our consciousness will belong to us and we will be free from the body of a human being. Yogis say we can do that. Sushumna yoga called it Brahmanadi, Mahapatha (Avenue), Shmashana (cemctery), Shambhavi (Durga), Madhyamarga (middle), Shaktimarga (Shakti path).

In addition to three main Nadis, there are some others were mentioned:

Gandhari: Left eye

Hastyihva: Right eyes

Pusa: Right ear

Yashasvini: Left ear

Alambusa: Mouth

Kuhush: Genitalia

Yhamkhini: Anal

There are Nadis down to the heels.

Mantrayana Buddha Yoga also has three vessels: Lalana, equivalent to Ida, it is Prajna. Rasana, equivalent Pingala means skillful means (upaya). Avadhuti is equivalent Sushumna which is the path to Nirvana, the middle.

The Nadis that were written in italics are in the astral form. They are drawn here equivalent to the same part of the physical body.

According to the Indian Hatha Yoga, the power of Kundalini was definite: Kundalini is the universal energy in the human body of each individual. It is not the physical power, such as electric or magnetic. Psychic powers, Shakti or universal powers have no shape. It is the holy Shakti that is sleeping in a circle in every human being. The mysterious Kundalini lies with the face down on the mouth of Sushumna Nadi. When it is awakened, it makes a hiss sound like snake, so it is also known as the power of the snake. Kundalini is the goddess of words and was praised by people. The Kundalini herself, when awakened, will give the yogi the enlightenment (Wisdom). Kundalini gives emancipation and self-knowledge. Kundalini is also called Saraswati because she is the source of all knowledge and bliss. Kundalini is pure consciousness, is Brahman, and is Prana Shakti, the supreme force. This world exists because of Shakti. All the creation, maintenance and disappearance take place in the Kundalini.

Kundalini yoga is an extreme meditation experience of Hatha Yoga. This practice is for the advanced yogis, under the guidance of competent teacher (guru). It requires the knowledge of the astral form and its structure, as well as both physical body and the astral form must be cleaned.

In Kundalini meditation, the sacred power of sleep in every human will be awakened and risen up through the chakras, or the spiritual centers of the body. At the top of the head, the place of highest consciousness, the unity of individual consciousness and the super consciousness will happen.

The balance of the universe is maintained by the Yin and Yang, men and women, and active and static. Anything that exists in the macro universe also exists in micro humans. Siva, the fundamental forces supposedly passive masculine or Yang, stays in Sahasara, the seventh chakra, located at the top of the head. Shakti, the feminine power and dynamic, lying in a circle in the end of spine, it is the apparition of universal energy in the body in the state of latent, dormant. It is not a physical power; it is the power, the spirit in all its pristine lying under organisms or minerals. Since this power starts moving spirally upward, like the power of snake, it is described by drawings of a snake lying in a circle in the base of the spine.

The Hatha yoga asana awakens Kundalini by the body discipline, cleansing the Nadi, and the astral channels that Prana flows through and control of Prana. The Hatha yoga asana will firm the nervous system. It allows the nervous system to withstand the rising energy experience. It regulates the flow of Prana in the locks, the mudras of the body, as known as mudra and bandha. Kriya is a specialized technique for cleansing the organs inside the physical body, and controlling breath to stabilize the mind. However, the powerful Pranayama, asana and meditation are not enough. The purification of the mind is required by us to serve not for ourselves, but for the community with pure a purpose. Kundalini and its moving channels are not found in the physical body. All parts of the physical body have an identical counterpart in the astral body, and both the bodies depend on each other in the physical realm. Seven spiritual centers, or chakras, Sushumna nadi, the channels that the Kundalini gives rise to, are in the astral body and equivalent to the nerve centers and spine.

According to the theory of yoga, there are about 72,000 nadis, astral neural tube, the most important of which is Sushumna nadi (the spine channel), the part of the physical body that is the same as astral body is the marrow. There are two nadis by its side called Ida and Pingala, equivalent with the sympathetic nerves of the left and right in the physical body. Prana, the vital energy, flows in them. As long as this vital energy still flows in Ida and Pingala, people also participate in the activities of the material world. We are bound by time, space and karma. However, when Sushumna of a yogi starts working, he will overcome such limitations. The spiritual practitioner has to have a thorough knowledge of the main nadi. The Sushumna nadi comes from the Muladhara chakra, located in the second vertebrae coccyx area, to Brahmarandhra, in the top of the head. The physical spinal cord was created by the gray and white matter of the brain (o-ras), and it is hung in the spine. In the spinal cord, there is an anatomy channel center.

There is another channel inside the red Sushumna, vajra, bright as the sun. This channel contains another channel called chitra with light pale color. Inside the chitra, there is a very small and very fine channel called Brahma nadi. When the kundalini is awakened, it moves in to this channel from Muladhara chakra to Sahasrara chakra. In this channel, there are major chakras. Each chakra represents a different level of consciousness.

Chitra nadi is the most important part of the body, and is sometimes called the 'heaven road'. The lowest part of Chitra nadi is the beginning of the Sushumna, which is called Brahma Granthi or 'Brahma stop'. The Kundalini will go through this stop when it rises up and upward to the end of nadi in the cerebellum.

VI. CHAKRA YOGA

The six chakras are six stops along the Sushumna; the last station is Sahasrara chakra. They represent different levels of consciousness and bliss. They are the places to reserve subtle Prana energy. They have the corresponding centers in the spinal cord and in the nerve centers of the physical body. Both have an intimate relationship. The vibrations in the physical centers by certain methods will create special effects as desired in the astral centers. The location of the chakras and their corresponding centers in the physical body are:

1. Muladhara: located at the lower end of the spine, corresponding to sacral plexus.
2. Swadhisthana: located at the genital area, corresponding to prostatic plexus.
3. Manipura: located at the navel area, corresponding to the abdominal plexus.
4. Anahata: located at heart area, corresponding to the cardiac plexus.
5. Vishuddha: located at the throat area, corresponding to the throat nerve plexus.

6. Ajna: located between the two eyebrows, trikuta, corresponding to the sinus plexus.

7. Sahasrara: located at the top of the head, corresponds to the pineal gland plexus.

While meditating, each chakra is envisioned as a lotus with a certain number of petals. The chakra Muladhara, Swadhisthana, Manipura, Anahata, and Ajna Vishuddha has four, six, ten, twelve, sixteen chakras and two petals corresponding to each chakra. The Sahasrara chakra has a thousand petals. The number of petals is determined by the number and the location of the nadis that are radiated from each, and it looks like the lotus flower. They droop down when kundalini does not work and the nadis will look up with the raise of kundalini.

Each petal will have one of the fifty Sanskrit letters that represent the vibrations of Kundalini when it passes through the chakras. These sounds existed in latent form. It will be expressed through the vibrations of the nadi and we can feel it while we focus. Besides the petals and the vibration of sound, each chakra has its own geometric shape representing a specific power, as well as its own color, its own function, one of five elements, its own God and bija and its own mystical vibration waves.

There are many ways to locate the chakras. All the chakras can be approached from the front and behind the back. It is easier for a beginner if you think Muladhara, Manipura, Anahata, and Ajna are the center point more than a focus point. When you can locate the chakras from your back, you can move your focus directly upward, along the spine, from this chakra to another. If you approach them from the front, you will move from the bottom of the spine to the navel, the heart, the throat and so on. You must stay aware from the inside and always receive the vibration experience that we feel inside to identify an energy center. You should have a comfortable meditation posture and keep the spine straight in all practices.

We can focus on these chakras and chant OM, the universal vibration sound, with different high and low tone. First, you focus on the chakra Muladhara with the lowest OM tone. Then move up the spinal cord to the next chakra, each time raising your voice higher until the OM sound gradually becomes imperceptible. There is another method to identify the location of the spiritual center, applying the scales of pitch of Indian music. There is a clear relationship between the scales of pitch and the chakras. 'Sa' corresponds with Muladhara, 're' with swathisthana, 'ga' with Manipura, 'ma' with Anahata, 'pa' with Vishuddha, 'da' with Ajna and 'ni' with Sahasrara.

When the Kundalini is awakened, it does not go straight up the Sahasrara unless that person is an extremely pure yogi. It must be moved from this chakra to others, and the yogi need to be extremely focused and patient. It could fall back and the yogi must put in a great effort to lift it up again. Even when kundalini is raised up to the Ajna chakra, it is difficult to keep it there. Only the great yogi such as Sri Ramakrishna, Sri Aurobindo and Swami Sivananda can keep it there as long as they want. When kundalini finally goes from Ajna to Sahasrara, the merger will happen. But it will not stay here for a long time. Only after long and continuous practice, the senior and pure guru can experience the eternal spiritual merger and final emancipation.

Kundalini can be raised quickly or slowly. It depends on the purity, the spiritual evolutionary state, the passion, the purification of the spiritual nerve and Prana covers, and the emancipated desire of the yogi. Then at the right time, Mother Nature will wake him up and give him the spiritual knowledge when he is ready. When he cannot fully absorb this spiritual knowledge, there are no profound important things that will be revealed to him.

There are countless physical and breathing practices to support the meditation on the chakra is emphasized that this meditation should be done under the guidance of a guru, and only after several months of purification and preparation. However, teachers cannot give students the necessary power or the self-discipline that should be achieved by him.

The Earth chakra

Muladhara chakra is located at the base of the spine. It has a square mandala representing the earth element, which is yellow, and the bija Mantra is lam. Four red lotus petals are attached to the vibrating waves of vam, sham, and sam. The bija Mantra start from upper right petal and will be chanted along right-hand direction. Lord Brahma is owner. In this chakra, the kundalini is sleeping. This is also Brahma granthi, or the stop of Brahma which will be opened through a high Sadhana and extreme purification to raise the kundalini up.

Meditating on Muladhara will bring knowledge of the Kundalini, and how to wake it up. It gives the mind and breath control and knowledge about the past, present, future.

The water chakra

Swadhishthana chakra is in the Sushumna located in the genital area. It controls the lower abdominal area, kidney, etc, in the physical body. Its element is water.

Meditation focuses on the crescent of this chakra and will bring the ability to control the water and given the spiritual power, the intuitive knowledge and knowledge of heaven. Many impurities will be eradicated.

The fire chakra

Manipura chakra is located in the Sushumna nadi, at the navel, and corresponds to the solar plexus. The red triangle mandala in the center of it contains the fire element.

The yogi who can focus on this chakra successfully will not fear fire and will not get sick.

The heart chakra

Anahata chakra is located in the Sushumna in the heart area. It does not belong to air or fire. It is in a smoky mandala and looks like the David star in the center of the chakra. The Bija mantra is yam. Twelve dark red lotus petals are represented by kam, kham, gam, gham, nam, cam, cham, jam, jham, tam and tham. The owner is Goddess Isha.

The Anahata sound is Sabdabrahman, the primitive sound, and can be heard in this chakra. Meditate on Anahata chakra will bring the pure virtue, compassion, and supernatural power.

The sound chakra

Vishuddha chakra is located in the Sushumna nadi at the bottom of the throat, and corresponds to the throat plexus in the physical body. It also corresponds to the fifth universe. It is in a pure blue circle. Its element is space (ether). The Bija mantra is Ham. Sixteen smoky purple petals contain Sanskrit vowels: am, am, im, im, um, um, rm, rm, Im, Im, em, aim, om, aum, am, ahm. The woner is God Sadasiva.

A yogi who can focus and meditate in this chakra will achieve higher success. He will receive the knowledge of the four Vedas and understand the past, present and the future.

The third eye chakra

Ajna chakra is in the Sushumna, which is between the eyebrows, trikuta. OM is the seed word for this chakra. It is the region of mind. It is found in a pure white circle. Each side of the circle has two lotus petals, white and pure, and its vibrations are represented by two Sanskrit sounds, ham and ksham. Its element is avyakta (mind). The clouds are a mix of primordial energy and material. The owner is God Paramasiva.

A yogi who can meditate in this chakra will eradicate his karma and become an emancipated soul. There is an intuitive knowledge through this chakra. This is where the power of the soul begins. Yogis intend to put their Prana in this place when they die. All the yogis, especially the Jnana Yoga yogis, focus on this chakra and chant the OM sound.

The crown chakra

Sahasrara is a subtle center that is located above and beyond the other six centers. All the other chakras have an intimate connection with this chakra. It is located on the top of the head, corresponding to the pineal gland of the physical body. There are a thousand petals. On each petal, there are fifty Sanskrit letters that are repeated. This is the residence of Lord Siva.

The top of the head is medically known as neonatal fontanelle. It also is called the Brahmarandhra, 'Brahma's hole'. When a junior yogi dies, they separate them from the physical body. It will open up and the Prana will escape through this chakra.

When the Kundalini Shakti merges with Siva at Sahasrara, the yogi will experience the ultimate bliss. He will reach the super conscious state and attain the most advanced knowledge. He will become a fully developed Jnani.

As noted above, the invisible lines (intellect sensations) are a network of subtle channels known as 'energy lines' (nâdis), through which the life force (Prana) circulates. It was shown through chakras practice according to the Kundalini theory. It is described in detail below:

'Energy' is an invisible force, 'line' as wire, visible fibers: it is called so based on concepts already available, such as 'light line' (spark), 'eyes's line' (glint of the eyes). But you must notice that the 'energy line' is invisible to human beings. Anatomy of Yoga physiology is not the result of an 'objective' search. It is self-awareness in each isolated individual. According to the Yoga discipline, the yogi has to observe the inner world (back to the inside) to review the inner incidents; it is not about operating the dead body, or observing the structure of the human or animal. We have to review and get our own experience from events and feel for ourselves. For example, when the yogi feels the warm flow moving inside the body, through the spine up to the jaw and the teeth become hard, he is coming into the Samadhi state.

The energy centers are also known as chakras (the Circle, Disc, center). It is the pure energy flow spinning in Nadi. There is a bright energy inside each chakra.

According to the Western concept, the brain is the only headquarters of knowledge. Yogis experienced that besides the brain, there are other centers in the body, along the vertical axis, which converge, exchange and distribute the energy flow (air). These centers are where the mind and body interact, and exchange the energy flow amongst each other. It means that the body will be back to the mind. The bright energy and mind energy are becoming the physical body and the body is becoming the mind energy. From this plexus look like the wheel; it is also called the petals of lotus (padma). Therefore, they are symbolized by the lotus flower with different colors and petals with 1 Sankrit sound on it, and symbol of their element and sound (mantra or bija) equivalent with one riding beast (vahana) that is contemporary expression the personality of their element.

There are seven main chakras that have been described shortly in a table; except for a few special chakras that require more detailed descriptions. According to the Hindu system, each chakra also is managed by a God, and will have one counterpart goddess (Shakti).

The first chakra: There is a yellow mandala inside a lotus. It represents the earth element (Prthivi). There is a triangle which is pointed against the ground (Yoni symbol) called Kamarupa. Inside the triangle is the penis (Svayambhulinga) with its head shining like a jewel. The lighting Kundalini is wrapped around Linga, sleeping, and her mouth gagged Linga so it closed the Brahmadvara (the gate of Brahman) that is also the gate of the Sushumna (also called Brahmanadi). Thus, this chakra is located in the start of the three nadis: Ida, Pingala, Sushumna, which probably means Kanda or called the Hui Yin in acupuncture.

The number 1, 2, 3, 4 chakra is represented for earth, water, fire, and wind element and its Sanskrit consonant. Number of lotus petals is from 4, 6, 10, and 12. It means that discrimination is increasing. The vibration, the rhythm and the level of activity has also increased as the character of the four elements, thus the consciousness level has also increased.

The fifth chakra, where the voice comes with the powers of the Mantra, contains all audio samples and a sophisticated expression of akasha and intermediate factor of audio vibrations.

The 7th Chakra, Sahasrara chakra, that should have been called sahasrarapadma, the thousand petals lotus with a thousand Sanskrit syllables on each petal which means there are every pronunciation of the Sanskrit form in it. But it can be gathered in one source sound OM. It is between the shower and combat face down with one round donut, in on triangle. The key here is the meeting place of Shiva and Shakti final (unmani) and where Kundalimi exits smoothly after the sixth chakra below.

The seventh chakra no longer belongs to the physical body. It is named on the super consciousness. Therefore, it explains why people often called the theory of 'six chakras'.

'The thousand lotus petals is at a higher level than the other six chakras. The word 'chakra' is no longer applied to it, thus, satcakramnupanam (6 chakras theory) is assigned to the Kundalini Yoga.'

After the Visudha (the fifth chakra), the cylinder and the spinal cord is over. The Sushumna bends forward and touches one point on the forehead, between the eyebrows: the Ajna Chakra, then it grabs momentum to go to the top of the head, a lump might be raised in this area, as known as the Buddha lump. For Daoism practitioners, the lump will be on forehead. The Buddha lump is not Sushumna as Buddha belief. It is only a sign that the practitioner had a super spiritual improvement. After breaking last frontier and glowing in this spirit status, I understand that Sushumna is the super consciousness (ultimate) which is dynamic and is caused by the sequential transformation of the spiritual potential through one process that Sahasrara is the ultimate ending. Any surpluses are the means.

The goal of Hinduism is the intercourse of Shiva and Shakti to experience the Satchitamanda. The goal of Buddhism is the emancipation (from ego-grasping), and experience the emptiness (Sunyata) rather than non-dual (Advaita) as Hinduism.

An Indian master, Sri Aurobindo said, 'The thousand petals lotus chakra is sometimes called the empty chakra (Shunya) because it is not in the body but in space above or over the physical head. It was the first step towards the tranquility of ego.

The discovery of the nervous system and blood circulation belongs to another era. The word 'energy line' was used in medical surgery in India later to show the nearest meaning of the word equivalent to veins or nerves (tendons). If we use this meaning for the primitive yoga terminology, it will not be justified. Many people who presented the 'Prana practice' (how to control the life force energy) have not seen that it is also a power which is not only being frequent changed but can also flow in multiple ways without any interruption. It is like an electric current that can run in copper, iron, water or silver. When the voltage is high, it can jump through space or be spread out by the waves. The mind power is similar; it can use the breath, blood and nerves. It may not need it or exit without these means, spread out into space and interact without space limitation because it is stronger than the breath, neural capacity, life-force of blood flow fecundity of semen, nerval movement reflection capabilities of the brain, or strength of the though. All these things are just the transformation of Prana, and the chakras are just the variations of the emptiness principle.

Sometimes, the yogis feel there is nothing left. This means that all their chakras have moved and the whole the body was cleared. They feel like nothing is moving in their body, but in fact, it was moved and has cleared the whole body. The energy flow will automatically and operate a natural way.

Thus, although the energy line may coincide with the nervous system, respiratory or circulatory and often can be compared with their function, the energy line and the function is not the same with them. It is also like the function of chakras to the organs and its physical function. In other words, there is a parallel between the physical and psychological function.

There is a way of expressing this parallel concept, that is the theory of five 'elements' of human consciousness. The five elements are possible to be solidified around or from a point in the deepest of our nature. It is the midpoint of the relationships where all internal forces are gathered. According to the Buddhist notion, the midpoint is empty; there is no characteristic or definition. One of the forms it was expressed is our body that was created out of food. There is another physical form which is more sophisticated, that is the ether. It is nourished by breath and travels throughout the whole body. We can call it the Prana. There is another more subtle form. That is the body created by our mind. We can call it consciousness. The fourth form is the hidden consciousness, beyond ideological activities; it is the subconscious that includes all the spiritual talents.

The seven chakras are the inner energy centers. If we open it up, the internal power is generated. We normally do not have the internal power, but when we open these chakras, we will have inner power and the body will change. When we can achieve it through practicing yoga, our vigor and strength will be generated that will bring us the intellect that we can apply it to our life. If you only have the intellect, you still cannot do anything if you are in hospital all day long to cure your sickness. You cannot do anything useful to help the community. So, you have to master your body first in order to apply your intellect to your life and serve the community. The Buddha's philosophy can open the intellect inside you, but for the body you will need yoga. Because of it, it opens the chakras to create a good health for the practitioner.

It is similar to Daoism. When the essence is burned finely and is moved from below the navel through the backbone (essence turn to pure air), it meets the Kundalini along the spine all the way to the shoulder. When it moves to the lumbar near your shoulder, you will hear the sound like 'crack'. It is the pure air turn to ether (pure air turn to energy). Then, it turns to o-ras (the subtle energy) that will nourish the brain cells that will improve your intellect.

The fourth element is the hidden knowledge, the 8th sense, our consciousness.

The final element is more sophisticated than the others and it is the deepest. It is called 'immaculate element', no more delusions, nourished by bliss, joy and peace of great supreme mind. This can only be known in the state of enlightenment, or in the highest peak of meditation. According to the Mahayana Buddhism, it corresponds to the sa-bhogakāya. The practitioner who achieves this state of mind will empty himself of all and be filled with bliss. It proved that Buddhism promotes our own internal resources rather than pray to get the external resources.

Thus, these elements cannot be understood as the separated classes that are located closely together on a solid center. These principles infiltrate each other from the most sophisticated 'brilliance everywhere', and scrutinize elements to the 'substance and consciousness' element that shows clearly in front of everyone; the most fully sophisticated element and the rawest conscious merger element.

Prana penetrates the body that is created by food and makes it work. Meanwhile, the mind penetrates the energy functions of the Prana and shape the physical manifestation. But thinking, breathing and body was infiltrated and provoked by consciousness that is even deeper than past experience. In this deep consciousness, there is hidden infinite material, as the source of ideas. Because we do not have a better way of expression, we call it the subconscious.

However, in an advanced state of meditation, all conscious (feeling) or unconscious functions (no feeling), exquisite, living or raw material were infiltrated and transformed by the fire of your breath in and immaculate peace until the pure consciousness revealed. The Kundalini practice (at the navel chakra) of Yoga is based on that progress. This will help the practitioner to regulate the entire body.

In conclusion, only the essence that is revealed through breathing practice (the fifth element, the immaculate element) can penetrates through the five classes and harmonize all the organs and individual aptitudes to become one. The secret of immortality is in this accomplishment. As long as we have not reached the fullness and we can self-identify with these 'parts' or inferior materials, we are still controlled by the laws of matter and the illusory realities. That is the law of death.

Nevertheless, it would be a misconception, if you underestimate the importance of the physical body that is created from food. Because, by its nature, it is being limited and hence will have no ability to penetrate the other 'elements'. The bodies become a theater for all mental events and of all decisions. We can say that the body is the stage that was created between heaven and earth to show the universal spiritual play. For the practitioner, it is a sacred arena of a deep and endless 'secret'. Therefore, the knowledge or awareness of physical experience is the most important thing for a guru, and for anyone who wants to follow the path of meditation. It is needed to understand the element of Prana in the breathing process, to raise the awareness of the importance of the body.

According to the Mantrayana Yoga, the guru will have to be responsible for 70% the success of the disciple. The guru and students have to share a deep understanding towards each other to be able to be indoctrinated and accomplished. The Kundalini discipline requested a competent guru to lead the students to open it, if they are not careful enough, the Kundalini will go the wrong way and can cause death to the practitioner.

The metabolism of your body comes from the internal energy emanating from the chakras. Ancient Buddhas also used the Toumo to create the energy.

Summary of yoga disciplines

This is a system of the Yoga discipline for a yogi who follows the Tantric Buddha. In terms of meditation, Raja Yoga (the sum of the three disciplines above) is an advanced discipline. The classic core part was described by Patanjali after researching and practicing, and a rare awareness.

A summary for all three disciplines, Kriya Yoga, Sushumna Yoga and Chakra Yoga. Despite being perfect on practicing these yoga disciplines, it only helps the yogis training their bodies and breathing come back to their inner pure consciousness, the

Buddha mind. The gurus who have experienced and achieved these Yoga disciplines can combine the three disciplines of yoga in their body. It saves time for the yogi and is an effective means for practitioners to have good and healthy, and internal power faster for his practice and service to the community.

VII. MEDITATE ON INNER SOUNDS METHOD

We have learned about the practice of Vajrayana yogacara meditation as the path to the Buddha mind and acquiring the wisdom through the eye-consciousness (eye sense). In all the consciousness, the eyes and the ears are the two most sensitive senses. Another way to practice awakening, awareness and intuition is through the ear-consciousness. That means we must return to listening to our own inner sounds.

We often hear about listening skills in communication. Listening skill is the most important to succeed in all conversations. There is an old Russian saying- Human beings take three years to learn to speak, but it takes a lifetime to learn to listen. However, here, I do not mention listening skills in ordinary communication. We learn about our ability to listen and observe our inner sound when we face the audible object.

When we face the sound, the ears help us receive the sound, the knowing in the Alaya consciousness helps us perceive that sound, and thoughts from our brain arise and create the feedback sounds in our brain. At this time, we have to be awake to listen to our own inner sounds. Among the inner sounds that are constantly created in our heads, what sound is from the True mind? What sound is the voice of the ego?

The important thing is that we must learn to listen to the inner voice. We must hear the sound of intuition that reminds us and not the illusionary ego. The best practice for developing our intuition is by listening to the inner sounds and feel the energy and go along with it. That is to listen to our body and feeling.

Our minds are often filled by the sounds of desire, love, hatred, judgment, future planning, suffering, regret, self-respect, low self-esteem and so on. But our souls notify us through two feelings: the state of relaxed bliss and the state of the unpleasant. If we often have a habit of observing the arising thoughts and feeling our state of the body, we will recognize what our intuition wants to tell us. So, we will never misunderstand the truth, we will have empathy and know how to behave properly. This is the peak of our ability to listen to the wisdom of our own pure mind.

Practice: For example, when someone says bad words to us, if we immediately respond furiously in the unconscious, we are being dominated by our uncomfortable feeling. We lose our awakening, awareness and intuition. If we want to have the wisdom or intuition from our own pure mind, we have to train ourselves a habit. It is the habit to recognize our feelings when listening to anything. When we begin to be awaked and aware of the information and emotions that come with it, our mind returns to a state of peace and purity. From this state, intuition shows a sound telling us how we should behave. If we listen to that sound, we are listening to the sound of our inner self and applying our own wisdom of our True mind.

So, the premium wisdom of listening is not listening to others but listening to ourselves.

The difficulties of listening to the inner voice:

Once upon a time, a very well-educated and erudite man came to see the Buddha. He asked Buddha a question.

Buddha replied: "*I cannot answer right now.*"

The man was surprised: "*Why can't you answer? Are you busy?*"

This was a noble man, well- known in the whole country, and of course, he felt offended by the fact that the Buddha was so busy that he could not spare a couple of minutes to answer.

Buddha replied: "*No, that is not the point. I have enough time, but you won't be able to comprehend my words right now.*"

He replied the Buddha: "*What do you mean?*"

Buddha said: "*There are three types of listener minds.*"

Buddha continued, "*The first listener's mind is like a pot turned upside down. No knowledge can enter that pot. The second listener's mind is like a pot with a big hole in it, wandering so much that all the knowledge leaks out immediately. In the third case, the listener's mind is full with other things; it can contain aggression, jealousy and destruction of all kinds. One has mixed feelings about what is being said and cannot really understand it. The pot is not turned upside down, and it doesn't have a whole in the bottom, but it has not been cleaned properly. You are the third type so it is difficult for me to tell you anything at the moment. You need to clean your mind first.*"

Through the story we see that there are three types of listeners minds that make it impossible for us to hear the true sound of our own Buddha nature. The first is that we do not listen or listen in the mind like a pot turned upside down.

The second is to listen in the mind of vague and unconcerned mind. We listen from ear to ear like a pot with a big hold in it.

The third is to hear in the mind of the ego, the attachment, like a pot full of impurities.

All three kinds of listener minds make us act unconsciously. In order to gain wisdom when we listen, we need to keep calm to listen and be aware of our own emotion.

VIII. SLEEPING MEDITATION TO DEVELOP WISDOM

We spend one-third of our lives sleeping. Sleeping time is the time for our body to recover our lost energy naturally. From a meditation practitioner's point of view, sleeping is a precious meditation period. Human beings often get lost in the unconscious when they fall sleep. However, a meditation practitioner who wants to practice awakening, awareness and intuition wisdom can practice meditation while he is sleeping to develop his wisdom. If we can go to a suitable state of meditation before we fall sleep, then we will be sleep derived. We will turn our sleeping time into a meditation period.

The evening meditation should be practiced by lying in bed before sleeping. After meditating, we only quietly fall asleep. This is the last thing we do on a day.

Practicing instruction:

Step 1: Relax your body

You need to lie down in a comfortable pose, such as the Savasana pose (lying on your back) or the reclining Buddha pose (lying on your right site). Being in a comfortable pose, our body should stay immobile. Parts of our body start to relax. Our mind focuses on observing our body so that it becomes more and more relaxed.

Step 2: Follow your breath

We will let our perception follow our breath, especially the abdomen breath. First, inhale gently, direct the breath to go deep down to the lower abdomen and feel your belly rise up. Then, exhale slowly and feel your belly flatten. Keep your breath calm and regulated. If you lie on your back, you can put your hands on either side. In order to feel your abdomen breath, you can put your right hand on your chest and your left hand on your belly if you are a woman, or counter the hands position if you are a man. If you have never experienced the abdomen while breath, you can place a small heavy object on your lower abdomen (like a brick or something have same weight) so that your body can automatically adapt to the abdomen breath automatically.

Step 3: Settle your mind.

When our body is relaxed and our breath is regulated, many thoughts come to our mind. As they come to us, we should let our mind focus on our breath. By doing so, our mind will not be distracted by the thoughts which can distract us or concern us. As a result, we will be able to achieve a deep and dreamless sleep.

Step 4: The natural awakening

When we practice sleeping meditation for a while, we usually fall asleep when our mind is following our breath. If we persistently practice sleeping meditation every night, our awakening wisdom will be developed naturally. In this stage, our mind and body are sleeping but our awareness is awake. We are still being able to acknowledge our breath and energy.

Step 5: The application of awakening, awareness, intuition when practicing sleeping meditation

The last thought of the night will become the critical idea in your sleep and the first idea in the next morning when you wake up. If you practice considering your past action on the last day and your future plan for the next day before practicing sleeping meditation, then you let go of everything, empty your mind and go to sleep. The questions you ask yourself about your problems before you fall asleep will be processed by your sub-conscious mind. It will automatically process the information without your mind. Your awakening, awareness, intuition and enlightenment will keep working when your body and mind are resting. They will give you the answer for your question after you wake up. By the time you wake up, your six senses (eyes, ears, nose, tongue, body and mind) are still in peace. At this time, if you lie calm and think about your tasks of the day, your will have the solutions for all of them come from your peaceful and insightful mind. It comes from the wisdom of the quiet mind or the Buddha mind.

PART IV
INSTITUTE OF VIETNAM BUDDHA YOGA RESEARCH AND APPLICATION

Institute of Vietnam Buddha Yoga Research and Application trains students on Buddha philosophy, yoga methods, and researches and applies biotechnology into the development of Vietnam Ngoc Linh ginseng.

Students are practicing in four schools: the family school, which is living by family love, being honest and compassion; wisdom school is to practice sacrifice, patience, diligence; the Buddha philosophy school and real life school by working in Ngoc Linh Ginseng Company and get paid.

1. How do students at the Institute practice?

Currently, yoga is being selected by the world as a training method for health. At Institute of Vietnam Buddha Yoga Research and Application, in addition to guiding the yoga methods such as Hatha yoga, Kriyâ yoga, Sushumna yoga, Chakra yoga, there is also the Buddha philosophy to focus the mind and apply it to life.

So how do we penetrate and apply the Buddha's philosophy to unleash our inner wisdom?

Here, we can learn anytime, anywhere, in every job and behaviors from smallest things to the bigger ones. We learn together through practice. All are becoming means to train the five mind sacrifices, patience, diligence, honesty and compassion that Buddha practiced and I also practiced to follow the scientific direction.

These five mind practices above are inner wisdom application. Here, as long as the practitioner knows how to apply the wisdom from the true mind. Every practice is intended to open and develop this wisdom.

The purpose of establishing Da Lat Buddha Yoga Center is for students to have real experience and application because learning must go together with the application. By doing and dealing with other people, we must use the five minds: sacrifices, patience, diligence, honesty and compassion.

2. Living environment and human behavior at the institute

We use honesty and compassion as a basis for dealing with people. In Institute of Vietnam Buddha Yoga Research and Application, we live together with the heart of honesty and compassion, work together with the mind of sacrifice, patience and diligence; living in solidarity and harmony will create a powerful resource.

In order to create a spirit of solidarity in the community, everyone must treat each other with honesty and compassion, do everything with a spirit of sacrifice, patience and diligence, and then the community will join together to become a powerful community, the power of love, of the true mind, the power of bright light.

If you think too much for yourself, it is selfishness; narrowness, jealousy, greed, and then the attachment and discrimination will appear and is saved into the mind to create resentments or the bad karmas. With such selfish living habits we will fail in life. On the contrary, if we always live with an honest and compassion heart, we will have many advantages; many people will support you on the way to be successful.

Each person comes here with different life circumstances and experiences, each person sincerely shares with each other about his or her life experiences, shares the difficulties in life, sacrificed his ego, be patience and diligently overcome all difficulties in life and work, it will create should one environment in which everyone gain their own understanding and skills.

3. Working mechanism of the institute

Here we do not have the management board. There is only the Master is the facilitator and we all live together and work in harmony with each other with sacrifice, patience, diligence, honesty and compassion. A harmony of honesty and compassion is a rare thing in this world which is full of lies and deceit. It is a gem that is more precious than anything. This is the "working mechanism" of two companies Vietnam Ngoc Linh ginseng joint stock Company and Thanh Quang Orchid Company and also the Institute. I consider all companies are just the means that I use to train Buddha Yoga students. It is a school that has both applied science and mind practice. Each person learns to the best of his or her own ability, does things that can harness the power available within him.

4. How to train Buddha yoga students?

This is an environment to train comprehensive students with healthy, skilled and prestige person. They know how to do everything by themselves, stand up and be mature in life, know how to organize at work, establish and run a company. When they are facing new problems and difficulties, they practice to be patient and seek solutions, capable of planning strategies and budgeting for projects. That is the lesson that comes from practice and application.

For the first example: I trained a student in the organization and administration skills during the construction of Da Lat Buddha Yoga Center. I observed my student dealing with his partners such as the director, the chief accountant, then the guard, the janitor. Then, he must lead the workers manage the communications and printing departments. He has to go to the transaction and buy goods by himself. Since then, this student has had skills at work and communication. By the practical work, the student learned how to use the money, how to save money, how to treat the agencies, organizations and individuals happy to collaborate with him to get the job done in the quickest, most effective way, setting up the strategy, organizing the work. He must learn to do all specific works of setting up a headquarters to the purchase of furniture and accompanying vehicles. That is the training human resource philosophy of Buddha Yoga, training a leader, a manager to know how to do everything, know how to strategize, how to treat people, master all situations, know how to sacrifice, patient and do your best to achieve your goals.

It is a transformation of the mind of a person who goes from a worker to become a leader, a master. Because one employee must be under the control and controlled of another and a leader will do it himself, decide for himself and handle everything, and coordinate reasonably to maximize the power and capacity of whole team. After a period of supervision, I hand over the work to the student to actively solve problems. After running the center, I give it to the student to manage themselves.

The second example: For example, a student of Buddha Yoga said, "Teacher, for technology and materials you can buy, but people you cannot buy." I think this student is right. When I gave difficult conditions that required this student to research and build Ngoc Linh ginseng production process based on nanotechnology although it was a completely new field for this student. For a short time, this student focused on research and gave the results back to me. That is proof that his words must be done. I continued to ask this student to do scientific research, collaborate and research with scientists to produce nanotechnology.

That is the orientation to train this student according to scientific research. I trained the student like this because I saw that his mind was honest and has a great heart. He was sacrificed, patient and diligent to complete the assigned works. That is the key that I gave to this student. Because he tried his best to complete the work, never refusing or complaining, I will continue to train this student to develop his skills with practical scientific research.

5. Operating criteria of the institute

"Continuously adjustment to survive and develop" is the operating criterion of the institute. If we work with honesty and compassion, we do everything in an economical and efficient way to reduce the cost and reduce the burden for organization. We have to know how to save all the resources, all costs in organization's operations, so that the organization is sustainable, economical and efficient production, and product costs is low to help consumers can purchase products. If a leader does not know such calculation, the consumers will have to suffer, how he can preach about honesty and compassion.

Therefore, the tagline of the Institute of Vietnam Buddha Yoga Research and Application is: "Earn money don't lose your true mind, use your money don't lose your true mind". How to make money without losing your true mind? The answer is your product has to be really good, economical; we earn money and use money to benefit the community, not for the individual.

BUDDHA YOGA CENTERS

Currently, the Institute has 4 free yoga centers:

1. 02 Buddha Yoga Center in Da Lat, Lam Dong province
2. Trung Kinh Buddha Yoga Center Hanoi
3. Vung Tau Buddha Yoga Center

Free Buddha yoga centers are established for students to practice the honesty and compassion heart. That is the application of inner power, mental power and wisdom power. By applying the Buddha's philosophy to daily yoga and work practices, each student will have his or her own health, skills, and prestige.

I am a teacher. I am in this world is not for doing business. I established companies as a means to train my students. We cannot be like the Buddha to bring a bowl to beg for alms, because this way is no longer suitable for today's science and technology era. Therefore, I use Ngoc Linh ginseng company as a means of training and application, rather than using Ngoc Linh ginseng for money. Although, in order to have a Ngoc Linh ginseng company like today, I had to climb up on 2800 meters high mountain to search for the precious ginseng tree, three times nearly lost my life in the mountains and countless hardships.

Our purpose has been set, we must go forward, try to overcome all difficulties and obstacles, even with only one last breath. In the last years of my life, I only had the sole goal of serving the community, helping the community gain health, skills and prestige.

Thus, Buddha's path is the scientific path. He practiced body and breath by yoga and the mind by applying sacrifice, patience and diligence into life. Buddha and yoga philosophy is a practical science. The centers are the application places to turn that these five mind into reality to achieve a peaceful and happy life right in this world.

Institute of Vietnam Buddha Yoga Research and Application

Director Prof. Dr Nguyen Van Sau
Most venerable Thich Hue Dang

Institute of Vietnam Buddha Yoga Research and Application was granted a certificate by Vietnam Ministry of Science and Technology (certificate number A-1693, issued on 27th December 2016), established under the decision number 1007/ QĐ-LHHVN on 19th December 2016 by Vietnam Union of

Science and Technology Associations. Most venerable Thich Hue Dang was pointed to be director. It was the first time Buddha philosophy and yoga was recognized by a highest scientific and technological management agency in Vietnam.

Activities in science and technology are follows:

- Study the philosophy of Vietnam Buddha Yoga, method exercises, routes of yoga practice in Vietnam and apply the philosophy and methods in improving skills, physical and mental health.
- Consult: train to improve human resources' capacity; organize scientific seminars, exchange the experiences to improve public health.

- Cooperate with domestic and foreign partners in order to conduct the tasks of the Institute.

- In addition to its headquarters, the Institute also established 04 free Buddha Yoga Centers in Vietnam, 01 Center in Hanoi, 01 Center in Ba Ria - Vung Tau, 02 Centers in Da Lat - Lam Dong to guide the community to practice yoga and Buddha philosophy to bring health - skills - prestige.

The Institute has cooperated with the Yoga Alliance in organizing the training 200h and 500h yoga teacher training courses according to international standards.

Contact:

Address: Tuyen Lam lake tourist area,
ward 3, Dalat city, Lam Dong province, Vietnam
Email: buddhayogavietnam@gmail.com

Trung Kinh Buddha Yoga Center in Hanoi

10 quotes to Create Their Values in Life Through Training Courses

1. You should practice and experiment the five steps: Sacrifice - Patience – Diligence- Honesty and Love to achieve yours's own wisdom.

2. Always controlling your mind with the path of awakening - awareness - intuition - enlightenment.

3. Treating others with criteria: "Taking the true mind as your father, taking wisdom as your mother, taking the community as your family" you will get prestige with a large community.

4. Health - Skills - Prestige are the most important criteria in every life, without one of these conditions, we cannot be happy.

5. Do not lose your true mind while earning, do not lose your True Mind while using money.

6. Knowing enough "Only people who knowing enough can live an honest life. If they do not know enough, their mind cannot be truthful."

7. The great true mind leads to great wisdom. The great wisdom leads to great virtue. The great virtue leads to great means. The great means leads to great prestige. The great prestige leads to great community. The great community leads great peace and happiness.

8. The dishonest life is a meaningless life / The dishonest work is immoral work / If you are not honest to yourselves you will not be honest to anyone.

9. Hardship is the step of success for intellectual ones, also the abyss for coward and lazy ones.

10. Continuous adjustment to survive and develop.

CONCLUSION

It is a difficult challenge to train a human being to get practical results. Human beings in any class, circumstance, any country, all need three basic things, which are: health, wisdom (skills) and prestige. If anyone in this world has these three treasures, he will surely succeed.

The practical results are a process of practice, apply into life and overcome countless hardships regardless of space and time.

A man needs good health to achieve skills in order to do all the work. These skills are gained by the light of wisdom. When we have health and skill, we can earn credibility for the work. And when we gain prestige, it also means that the arduous practice process has been rewarded with practical results and have benefited the community. That is proven through my life.

1. More than 20 years ago, I started to grow Cymbidium. I began to think about applying tissue culture method by myself to propagate the growth of orchids. Without any background in science, I self-studied books and consulted some experienced acquaintances. Getting back to Da Lat, I further researched and began propagating the orchids by the tissue culture method all by myself. Gradually, I created and controlled my own seedlings. Every year, I distributed Cymbidium throughout the country.

2. In August 2008, when I was nearly 70 years old, I decided to go with two students of mine to Ngoc Linh Mountain in Kon Tum province to find the natural Ngoc Linh ginseng. The Ngoc Linh Mountain is 2800 meters high which has a very tough terrain. I was exhausted, nearly fainted three

times. Overcoming many difficulties, at last, I obtained 98 natural ginseng plants in order to be the samples of breeding experiments. After many experiments, I, along with my students, successfully produced the product extracted from Ngoc Linh ginseng biomass in the form of tablets. I completed the production process and registered necessary legal procedures to ensure the quality of products before sending the product to the patients. This product has currently been serving many patients across the country in support of the treatment of many diseases, especially those related to liver, lung, diabetes and cancer.

3. I have practiced the three advanced yoga disciplines: Kriya Yoga, Sushumna Yoga, Chakra Yoga for nearly 50 years. Those are three yoga disciplines that have nearly been lost in the world today.

- The International Sivananda Yoga Vedanta Center under the Vedanta Forest Yoga Academy (headquartered in Quebee Jot 2Ro, Canada) granted me the title of Master of Yoga and Swami yoga according to Veda sutra.

- Establishing 04 Buddha Yoga Centers in Vietnam, 01 center in Hanoi, 01 center in Ba Ria - Vung Tau, 02 centers in Da Lat - Lam Dong to organize the training in 04 steps: Student - Teacher - Trainer - Senior Trainer - Master.

- Cooperating with the Yoga Alliance in the training of teachers and trainers of Vietnam Buddha Yoga according to international standards.

- In 2017, the Institute of Vietnam Buddha Yoga Research and Application cooperated with the Yoga Alliance to establish the Yoga teachers training for 200h and 500h according to international standards.

4. I was recognized as the lecturer of Propagation of faith (Buddhism) of Vietnam Buddhist Sangha under the document No.1941/GCN/BHP/HDTS dated August 24, 1999 of the Management Board of Vietnam Buddhist Sangha (Attached document in appendices).

I graduated the advanced course of the Central Dharma Propagation Committee of the Vietnam Buddhist Sangha. Graduation date: 28 December 2004, course time: 2001 – 2004

I have written and published 43 Sutras Lecturing sets and Sutras Interpretation books approved and licensed by Vietnam Religion Publishing House.

Currently, the Institute of Vietnam Buddha Yoga Research and Application is in Lam Dong, Tuyen Lam Lake tourist area. I am training 45 engineers. From 4:30 am – 8:00 pm teaching our students abo meditation. They implant tissue and make Ngoc Linh ginseng tablets in factory. They also learn yoga and Buddha philosophy. Then I trained the students to practice teaching the Buddha philosophy to the community.

I created an environment with five steps:

The first step: Students who come here to study can work at my company and get paid. Most of them are engineers who have graduated from universities. Therefore, they can practice their professional skill and earn a living. I pay the students 4 million to 7 million VND/person every month. In addition, all expenses of electricity, water, living, lodging, and clothes are all taken care of so that the students can be assured to work and practice.

The second step: Students can approach the high-tech working environment to produce the Ngoc Linh ginseng tablets. Carrying out scientific researches helps students gain wisdom.

The third step: Students practice yoga for health and inner strength. I collaborate with Yoga Alliance for yoga teacher training coaches, who are internationally certified. They practice and bring their training skills to the community at the Buddha Yoga Centers free of cost that I have set up all across the country.

Step 4: They practice listening to philosophy and teaching the Buddha philosophy. It is this step that helps them cultivate an open-minded thought process and do everything for their own benefit and for that of the community. This step is a step of opening the Buddha's wisdom for them, helping them have a clear vision and direction for their lives. This step in Buddhism is called the Bodhisattva path.

The fifth step is the way of applying wisdom for the development of the community, developing the nation's treasure ginseng, developing a healthy community by practicing yoga, and developing and building prestige in the country by application of 5 sacrifices - patience - diligence - honesty and compassion. This step in Buddhism is called Bodhisattva actions.

I use the company as a means to train skilled people and build careers for students.

I am taking yoga as a means for the practitioner to be healthy.

I take Buddha's philosophy to do things with a great heart and wisdom.

Thus, I have presented the purpose of life and the meaning of my life that can only be achieved when I have these three invaluable assets: HEALTH - SKILLS - PRESTIGE.

If human beings have health, they can apply their wisdom to have skills. When they have skills and then contribute to the community, they will gain prestige. I hope everyone can have prestige with family and community to contribute towards the development of the country.

Thanks to these three resources, my life is valuable and I can leave the community with valuable results. The first is to leave a work, the second is to leave a precious tree and the third is to leave a school for young generations to follow the path of practice and achievement.

In my career of training people, I always consider how to train them to be successful; How to train people gain wisdom; How to train them to go on the way which they have come through; How to train students to practice the five Buddha minds: sacrifice, patience, diligence, honesty and compassion; and how to create practical results and achievements and bring more and more benefit to the community?

The final dream of my life is to train people who can achieve wisdom and practical results. I joined the World Records Union with the desire to train people for the record holders. I want to collaborate with the World Records University to set up a Practical Results University to train record holders health and wisdom, and achieve practical results for Vietnam and the rest of the world.